THE UTAH HOA HANDBOOK

The Ultimate Guide to Homeowners' Associations for Buyers, Owners, and Boards of Directors in the State of Utah

Maxfield
COMMUNITY MANAGEMENT

ISBN: 9798328210874

TABLE OF CONTENTS

INTRODUCTION

You are reading this book because you are either a director for your association's board, an owner (or member), or a buyer considering purchasing a property in an association. The one common denominator is the existence of a homeowners' association, and you are a part of it.

This book is specifically designed for communities located within Utah.

Homeowners' associations in Utah are regulated differently than Condominium Associations. HOAs are subject to the Community Association Act, while condo associations must follow the Condominium Ownership Act. Both acts are similar to specific regulations regarding managing single-family homes or condominium buildings.

Most common interest communities, whether single-family homes or condominiums, choose to be registered as nonprofit corporations and are subject to the Utah Nonprofit Corporation Act.

This book is presented for educational purposes and is not meant as legal, accounting, or other professional services advice. The author makes no representation or warranties of any kind, and neither the author nor the publisher shall be held liable or responsible to any person or entity concerning a loss incurred or damages caused by the information presented in this book. Every homeowner is unique, and every buyer, association member, and board member should use their research and due diligence before deciding.

ABOUT ME

I am Derek M. Seal, and I was first licensed in 1992. and have been a licensed real estate broker since 2007 and have helped others sell and buy over nine hundred (900) properties in Utah from Logan to St. George and some in Arizona. My achievements earned me the prestigious Utah County Rookie of the Year title!

But my love for real estate doesn't stop at sales. I've also dabbled in property development and construction and creating remarkable properties. In 2008, I ventured into property management, starting Expert Property Management, which has since transformed into Maxfield Property Management. With over 900-unit years of experience (yes, that's a lot!), we expertly handle residential properties across Utah.

Expanding my horizons, in 2019, I founded Maxfield Community Management. We manage several small to medium-sized associations, ensuring smooth operations and happy communities. Sharing my knowledge and passion, I've had the privilege of writing articles, speaking at national conferences, and teaching continuing education classes for the Rental Housing Authority of Utah (formerly known as the Utah Apartment Association).

Education has played a vital role in my journey as well. I earned my BA degree in Marketing in 2002. I have more than 25 real estate related designations, of which the CPM® (Certified Property Manager) and MPM® (Master Property Manager and the CRMC® are the ones that mean the most. I have served as a national ambassador for NARPM® (National Association of Property Managers), past president of the Utah Chapter of NARPM®, and on several task forces. I currently serve on the Rental Housing Association of Utah (RHA) board of directors.

Now, my wife often reminds me that I downplay my achievements. Perhaps it's because I'm not one to boast, but I hope it reflects my genuine passion for property and community management.

Now, when I'm not immersed in the exciting world of real estate, you can find me enjoying quality time with my amazing wife and our three kids, who are still at home. We're a fun-loving bunch who love to travel and, of course, indulge in delicious food. With a family as large as ours (nine kids!), I've learned a thing or two about managing different personalities and creating a harmonious environment for everyone.

Enough about me, let's talk about Home Owner Associations.

SECTION 1

HOA BASICS

"Reading is the basics for all learning."

George W. Bush

What Is an HOA?

HOA stands for Homeowners Association. It is a legal entity created by a real estate developer or a community of homeowners within a specific residential area or housing development. The purpose of an HOA is to manage and maintain common areas and amenities and enforce clear rules and regulations within the community.

While there are two common types of HOAs in Utah - HOAs that are subject to the Community Association Act (HOAs) and HOAs that are subject to the Condominium Ownership Act (COAs), both are similar, but there are some differences. I will point out some of the differences along the way.

You automatically become an association member when you purchase a property within a neighborhood or community governed by an HOA. You must pay regular fees, known as HOA dues, to cover the costs associated with maintaining the shared facilities and services. These dues can vary depending on the neighborhood and the amenities provided, such as landscaping, road maintenance, security, recreational facilities, or shared utilities.

HOAs typically have governing documents, including bylaws, covenants, conditions, and restrictions (CC&Rs). These documents outline the rules and regulations that homeowners must adhere to, such as architectural guidelines, landscaping requirements, pet restrictions, noise regulations, and other community standards. The HOA is responsible for enforcing these rules and can impose fines or legal action against homeowners who violate them.

HOAs also often have a board of directors, typically comprised of homeowners elected by the community. The board is responsible for managing the association's finances, making decisions regarding the community's maintenance and improvement, and addressing homeowner concerns or disputes.

While HOAs can provide benefits such as well-maintained common areas and amenities, they also have limitations and potential drawbacks. Some homeowners may find the rules and regulations too restrictive or disagree with the decisions made by the HOA board. Even the insurance company Geico highlighted by exaggerating some persons sentiment about HOAs (Geico Commercial). I don't disagree with their parody; however, I think there is a lack of understanding and another reason for this book. Additionally, HOA dues can be an ongoing financial obligation that homeowners must budget for alongside their mortgage and other expenses.

It's essential to thoroughly review the HOA's governing documents, rules, and financials before purchasing a property in a community governed by an HOA to ensure it aligns with your preferences and lifestyle; if you are still reading this, you probably live in an HOA.

Who Is a Member?

Members of a homeowners' association are the owners of the individual units or lots, and the terms "members" and "owners" are used interchangeably in this book and most governing documents. A member is like a corporation shareholder and has certain rights, like voting for board members, access to the common areas, and the right to inspect association documents.

The member contributes a monthly assessment to the association (called dues). These pay monthly operating costs such as landscaping, insurance, and shared utilities. A portion of the dues are put in reserves (similar to a community savings account) to be used in the future to repair common area systems such as roofs, streets or even replastering the pool.

Some people may not realize that many Homeowner Associations register as non-profit corporations. A non-profit corporation, often simply referred to as a non-profit, is a type of legal entity formed for purposes other than generating profits for its owners or members. These organizations are recognized and regulated by laws in various countries and are subject to specific rules and regulations that differentiate them from for-profit businesses. HOAs that register as a non-profit in Utah are subject to the Utah Nonprofit Corporation Act as well as the other HOA and COA laws.

Why are HOAs Required?

The first homeowners' association in the United States comprised Saint Louis, Missouri's private streets and neighborhoods. Benton Place in Saint Louis opened in 1867, and the covenants, conditions, and restrictions (CC&Rs) of these intimate neighborhoods mandated that the homeowners owned the streets and the water and sewer lines. Some of the early associations in Los Angeles were established to create deed restrictions limiting property ownership to exclude non-Caucasians or non-Christians. Today, you can't exclude people based on the seven (7) federally protected classes and two (2) state-protected classes: Race, Color, Sex, Religion, National Origin, Disability, Familial Status, Sexual Orientation, and Gender Identity. Now, associations are formed seemingly to improve property values and provide the owners with a better quality of living. Cities prefer owners to reduce the burden on city services and transfer some responsibilities and liabilities to the home owners such as road maintenance which includes liability for additional sewer, gas and water lines, snow removal and as well as maintaining those park strips outlining a community.

The History of HOAs in Utah...

Homeowners Associations (HOAs) have a significant presence in Utah, and their history in the state dates back several decades. Here is an overview of the history of HOAs in Utah:

1. **Emergence in the 1960s:** HOAs began gaining traction in the 1960s in the United States as suburban development expanded across the United States. Utah, experiencing similar growth in housing communities,

established several early HOAs during this period.

2. **Legislative Framework:** In 1954, Utah enacted the Utah Community Association Act, which provided a legal framework for forming and operating HOAs in the state. This law established guidelines for creating, governance and enforcing HOAs and their regulations.

3. **Growth in the 1980s and 1990s:** The popularity of HOAs continued to rise in Utah during the 1980s and 1990s, fueled by increasing residential development. Many new housing communities, particularly planned developments and condominium complexes implemented HOAs to manage shared amenities and maintain community standards.

4. **Expansion of Powers:** Over time, the powers granted to HOAs in Utah expanded. In 1998, the Utah Supreme Court ruled in favor of HOAs, stating they had the authority to regulate architectural standards and enforce restrictions outlined in their governing documents.

5. **Increasing Influence and Regulation:** As the number of HOAs in Utah grew, so did their influence on residential communities. Homebuyers became more aware of the existence and implications of HOAs when purchasing properties. The state legislature enacted additional laws to protect homeowners' rights and promote transparency in HOA operations.

6. **Legislative Revisions:** In 2008, Utah revised its community association laws by passing the Utah Condominium Ownership Act. This act established guidelines for condominium associations, addressing issues such as board governance, financial management, and dispute resolution.

7. **Legislative Revisions:** In 2023, there were updates on which records an Owner is entitled to see under the Nonprofit Act. The law prohibiting an association from requiring an owner to rent out their home to pay an additional assessment or fee was modified to allow up to a $250

price if the association permits at least 35% of the units to be rental units. Other changes allow HOAs to disqualify individuals from serving on the board of directors if they have been convicted of a felony or are on the sex offender registry. Also, HOAs must allow political signs but can limit their time, place, and manner of posting.

It's worth noting that while this overview provides a general picture of the history of HOAs in Utah, specific details and experiences may vary across different communities and regions within the state.

Why Are HOAs Ever Increasing?

There are two significant reasons for the proliferation of HOAs since the early 1980s. One is specific to Utah, and the other is a nationwide trend. First, land prices have increased, causing single-family home prices to increase substantially, and a segment of buyers prefer higher-density housing near downtown areas. There has been a transition away from single-family detached homes, the dominant residential development trend in the country.

Developers traditionally focused solely on building and selling single-family detached homes as fast as possible to make a profit. They should have concerned themselves with building public amenities like parks. They assumed that city governments would tax new residents to create such things. By the 1970s, developers mainly needed more suitable land for such low-density developments.

They began to focus on building higher-density stories, often on marginal land that had been previously overlooked because it had been considered to be too rugged or too distant from urban downtowns. To make these developments profitable while complying with local density restrictions (which usually measured density in terms of average numbers across an entire story), they would often build high-density structures on one parcel, such as a condo complex, a cluster of townhouses, or a line of patio homes with zero lot lines (all of which require less sprawling infrastructure than the equivalent number of single-family detached homes it would take to house the same number of people).

They would simultaneously set aside an adjacent parcel to be left undeveloped as open space or developed into a recreational area like a park to benefit and serve the development's residents.

But first, developers needed to find a way to ensure that the inhabited parcels benefiting from the adjacent recreational areas would take care of them. Second, in Utah, increasing budget shortages made local governments eager to find ways to decrease expenses and increase revenue. This caused local governments to be increasingly reluctant to approve new residential developments since there was uncertainty about their ability to provide adequate public services to new residents based on current or future projected revenues.

HOAs transferred some of the responsibility for streets, sewer lines, water lines and streetlights, snow removal, street sweeping, and more from city-provided services to services that would be shared among the members of a particular community. Cities dangled increased densities (the ability to build more homes on the same land as long as developers created these Owner Associations that would assess homeowners to pay for such services.

What Are the Pros of HOAs?

❖ Ample Amenities

If you own a $3-5 million dollar home in Utah, you can afford an Olympic-sized pool, a tennis court, and a secure gated entry. If you are in the market for a $500,000 home, expect a place to sleep and eat only if it is part of a homeowners' association. I live in a master planned HOA that will have more than 1200 homes, and we have (at least that's what they promise) all those amenities, but I only pay for 1/1200 of them. We can afford these amenities by pooling our resources and splitting the costs. Some communities have private golf courses, security guards, extravagant clubhouses, and fitness facilities that rival luxurious hotels, which would otherwise be out of reach for an individual homeowner outside of an association.

❖ Utility Hacks

Community fiber internet is one of the best hacks that piggyback on the ample amenities. Suppose that Google or Xfinity wants to charge you $100 monthly for one gig of fiber internet. A community can request a bulk bill and get the same service up to 70% off. That makes those monthly dues a little more palatable. If you have questions about this simply give us a call.

Another utility hack that doesn't benefit everyone is combined utilities. If you have a larger household or like long showers, you may get a slight benefit of a lower utility bill.

❖ Increased Property Values Because Your Neighbor Cannot Paint Their House Pink.

An annoyance in neighborhoods without rules and regulations is an owner's ability to ruin the entire community's aesthetics because of their bad taste and drive down real estate values. Just go through the older streets of Salt Lake City (especially west of I-15), American Fork, Lehi, or Pleasant Grove, and you know what I mean. (Sorry to the people that live there - but I am only being honest.) The only "rules" a homeowner must adhere to are the local compliance laws their city regulates. Most requirements are broad, and it usually takes a town a long time to take action. In many cities, the grass can get long and weedy, or cars being worked on until the town gets involved.

Every association differs in terms of the number of rules and regulations and the board's commitment to force owners to adhere to those rules; some are very strict, and some are more lenient. Associations with architectural limitations or approval processes ensure that the exterior of properties conforms to a community standard, and owners can only make improvements or changes to the surface of their properties with board approval.

In a community of tan homes, one owner cannot decide to paint their house pink.

❖ Common Areas Uncommonly Clean

Since the association maintains the common areas, there is consistency in the community. One of the most significant expenses for a community is usually landscaping. Boards go to great lengths to find a company that will care for the lawns and trees to maintain the beauty of the community. Not only are the yards maintained, but also the exterior paint, roofs, siding, and anything else that is the financial responsibility of the association, as spelled out in the governing documents.

❖ No Need to Save for a Rainy Day

Every association uses monthly assessments to pay for the current operating expenses, and a portion of these assessments are put into a reserve account to pay for future payments. It is a forced savings plan for every owner. For owners not in an association, if the roof needs to be replaced, the roofer will want $10,000 to 15,000, and there is no payment plan. If an association is responsible to maintain the roof tops, and the board has adhered to the recommendations of the reserve study, there should be ample funds on hand to handle the expense of replacing the roof without the need for a special assessment or loan.

❖ Tenants Must Toe the Line

When an owner without an association turns their property into a rental, there is little to stop the tenant from running amok. If the owner does not hire a management company—and almost 70 percent do not—the tenant makes the rules. They may say "no pets" on the application and turn the place into a doggy daycare. They may say only three adults would live in the property, but then try to squeeze another three adults in to share the rent burden. The tenant is held to the same rules as the owner in an association. If they do not toe the line, the owner will be fined and reminded of this fact.

Some people won't consider buying in a homeowners' association, and many owners in an association won't buy again in one. So, what are the cons?

What Are the Cons of HOAs?

❖ Cannot Paint Your House Pink

Some people want to express their aesthetics through their property. They want a blue exterior and a red door. Even though, in most cities, there is no limit to your color choices. Once, a person in a town hung brass instruments in his front tree for twenty years. You guessed it: he taught band at the local high school, and when students hung up their device of choice, he hung them up in his tree for all to see. This would not happen in any association I am aware of. Many think it is their American right to do with their property as they see fit, as long as it complies with local ordinances, and no one can tell them otherwise.

❖ Heavy-Handed Owners - The Enforcers Extraordinaire

Ah, the heavy-handed owners in HOAs! They've taken rule enforcement to a new level, making the Gestapo look like a bunch of laid-back pals. They roam the neighborhood with cameras, documenting every minuscule violation like neighborhood paparazzi. Forget a friendly chat or a gentle reminder; they're ready to report even the tiniest transgression quicker than a caffeine-fueled cheetah.

It's like a reality show waiting to happen - "Altercations in the Hood!" Verbal battles and even physical confrontations become the highlight of the day. Who knew neighborhood disputes could be such thrilling entertainment? These rule vigilantes have traded peaceful coexistence for a boxing ring, all to enforce regulations with a personal touch.

But wait, there's more! Some owners believe they are the true rulers of the community. Who needs a management company when they can take matters into their own hands. They'll rewrite the rulebook, molding the neighborhood according to their whims and fancies and even refusing to raise dues to cover expenses. After all, what's more important than making the community cater to their personal preferences, even if it means turning off potential buyers and bankrupting the HOA?

❖ Not All Can Visit the Pool When It Is 100 Degrees Outside

Your community may have excellent amenities, but you may find that everyone wants to play tennis in the morning when it is cool and frolic in the pool when it is hot in July. Several HOAs have one collection of amenities and two to three hundred owners. Now not all owners will descend at once on the amenities but if thirty or fifty owners and their guests descend on the pool, that may take away the enjoyment of swimming there. It's similar to my recent cruise to Coco Cay, the private island of the Royal Caribbean Cruise Line in the Bahamas. Imagine 3000 guests descending on one big pool, one island at a time. That works out fine, however they seem to forget to tell you need to tell you that they dock three ships at a time some days, and then there are 12,000 guests using the same facilities.

❖ Tennis anyone?

My wife's parents live in Pepperwood, one of Utah's only gated communities- it has two guard stations, one pool, several tennis courts, parks, and walking trails. Guess how many times my in-laws have gone to play tennis? Yep, never, not even once in the 15 years they have lived there. One of the cons to an HOA is that you may end up paying for something you never use. Even if you never play tennis, you are paying for the resurfacing of the courts every ten years and the new nets, but at least it's a selling feature when you go to sell.

❖ Paying Monthly or Special Assessments Is Mandatory

There may be times when money is tight. While most of the HOA dues are for services, a portion is for capital expenses such as a roof replacement, replacing dead trees, and painting the exteriors. If the association hasn't collected enough reserves, the board may levy a special assessment to help "raise money" for those overdue repairs. I have seen special assessments easily be $1,000 to $5,000, and in one case, the developer of the complex made some huge building mistakes, and each owner had a $25,000 to $50,000 assessment, depending on the building they lived in. In these situations, some companies loan the money to the HOA and then collect a fee over the monthly assessment. Paying your monthly dues is the only option. You will incur late costs and interest on the unpaid balance if you do not.

If you do not pay your dues, the Board may have the management company issue you a pre-lien letter, and if you still refuse to pay, the board will authorize a lien to be placed on your property, for which you will be billed. As a measure of last resort, the association in which you live can foreclose on your property to recover their dues. The fees and legal costs can easily exceed the delinquent dues. Adding insult to injury, since you are no longer a member in good standing, the board can only allow you access to the amenities.

❖ You Pay for Your Neighbors' Water Bill

In some communities, you pay for the water bill for the common areas and individual owners. This bill is not prorated for each owner; the total water bill is divided evenly. So, if your association has an owner who likes to take hour-long luxurious showers, or there are just two people in your household, but the neighbor has their daughter and family living with them for the summer, you are paying for that.

❖ Equal But Not Equal?

Some owners get the benefit of improvements before others. For example, in my last association, they were repainting faded buildings. It is being done in phases to mitigate the cost. Some owners benefit from new paint, while others must wait even a few years. Monthly assessments are collected equally but spent unequally.

❖ The Bottom Line…

Homeowners' associations are here to stay. About 28% of homes in Utah are part of an HOA and that number is increasing. Increasingly, cities approve new communities only if an association governs them since they face increasing service costs and want to shift that burden elsewhere. Not only do cities prefer associations, but owners do, too. A research study 2005, "What are Private Governments Worth?" by Amanda Agan and Alexander Tabarrok, found that community associations add a 6.1 percent increase in property values over similar homes in nearby non-association communities. In Utah, where the median sales price in 2023 is $478,000, properties in associations sell for almost $30,000 more than comparable non-association homes.

This is remarkable because owners in associations pay the same property taxes as non-association owners and pay monthly assessment fees to maintain their community. Many association members indeed view the assessments as another bill they must pay for which they are not receiving anything of value. But as this study shows, the restrictions that come with an association, and the amenities that many associations include, protect the overall importance of the community.

The standards in an association's governing documents ensure the association's common areas are properly maintained and restrict activities that may hurt property values. Most members see the association's amenities as a net positive and do not envy that part of the assessment going to upkeep. Once the installation and continuing maintenance costs of most significant amenities are considered, there is a huge savings over an individual member solely purchasing most amenities. Ultimately, associations create higher home value and a more excellent quality of life for the owners.

SECTION 2

---◆◆◆◆---

INFORMATION FOR POTENTIAL
AND
CURRENT OWNERS

"You are not buying a house, you are buying a lifestyle."

Anonymous

What Should Future and Current Owners Look for in an Association?

Some buyers are in an association, and some owners wish they had researched more before moving into one. Let's analyze what to look for in an association to ensure it is a good fit if you are buying and then how to maximize your dues and rights if you live in one.

What Should You Look for When Buying?

Before even buying in an association, make sure you are comfortable abiding by the rules and regulations of any association. If you have too many vehicles, want to raise animals, or live to paint the exterior of your properties in primary colors, no association may be a fit for you. Regardless of the economic health of the association or how stringent the rules are, you may want to steer clear of buying any real estate in an association. But if a property's price, amenities, and location appeal to you, and you have decided to believe in an association, here is the due diligence you want to do to avoid conflict in the future.

❖ Inspection

It is no longer "buyer beware" when you purchase real estate. You have the right to inspect the property and receive pertinent disclosures from the seller. Your intent at the inspection is to determine what items the seller covers and what is included in your assessments. Is a plumbing leak your problem, or did the association repair it? Is a roof leak your responsibility or considered part of the common area? You can ask the seller or the management company for this information. During the due diligence period you may want to investigate if there is any pending HOA litigation as many communities have ongoing litigation, and any litigation must be disclosed to a buyer.

In Utah, a builder typically warrants the construction for one year but can be liable for construction defects for up to six years from completion, which is the statute of limitations. There may be construction defects soon after completion, or, as is more commonly observed, a law firm will reach out to an association before the six-year expiration and offer to examine the community and if there is any potential recourse against the builder for poor construction. If the HOA sues and wins damages, the attorneys earn a nice legal fee, and the community has funds to fix the issues discovered by the firm.

Some lenders will not lend in communities amid this litigation. In contrast, others will want to review the lawsuit to determine if the issues discovered impact the property's marketability. Sometimes, the litigation could be for one unit where the owner is suing the association to repair their unit, not community wide.

❖ Governing Documents

The seller or an escrow company will provide the association's governing documents, including CC&Rs, by-laws, minutes, articles of incorporation, and rules and regulations. Read these documents. Yes, they are boring, but as the name indicates, they will govern you and your property. Pay particular attention to the rules and regulations. These are the documents that govern your day-to-day behavior.

> ➢ What are the parking limitations?
> ➢ What are the pet restrictions?
> ➢ Are there Rental Restrictions?
> ➢ What improvements are you allowed to make?

The CC&Rs will usually be lengthy, and the language can be arcane, but this will spell out what expenses the association is responsible for and the owner's responsibility. The minutes record actions taken by the board at every meeting and may reflect the current issues facing the community.

❖ The Financials

Just as profits and losses provide insight into the economic health of a business, the financials do the same for your association. You will be provided a copy of the current year's budget, which will show variances from the expected expenses and any "surprise" bills. The balance sheet will reflect the cash on hand for the association in both the operating and the reserve accounts. The **reserve study** will show what the expert believes the association needs to pay for future repairs and replacement of major systems in the common areas. Very few, if any, associations are at 100 percent of the reserve—many are at 50 to 75 percent—and if the account is only at 20 to 30 percent of the recommended amount and future repairs are imminent, it could mean that, when you become an owner, you may face significant increases in the dues or a special assessment to pay for these repairs.

They may be able to take from one reserve account to pay for a project, **but even if you rob Peter to pay Paul, you still owe Peter**. Also, if there is barely enough money in the reserve accounts for the expected expenses, funds may not be available for the unexpected. If the community you buy in is thirty-plus years old, there will be unforeseen costs as the buildings and their systems reach their economic life.

❖ **Extra Credit**

Even though the seller is legally obligated to disclose all material issues with the property, what is material to one person could be insignificant to another. Talk to people who live in the community because they do not have a financial interest in your transaction. When doing the physical inspection, or at any point before removing contingencies, knock on the neighbors' doors. Tell them you are considering buying in their community, and ask the following questions:

> ➢ What do you like best about the community?
> ➢ What do you like least?
> ➢ If you could go back in time, would you still buy in the community?
> ➢ Any issues with any neighbors?
> ➢ Are there any unresolved issues in the community?

If you are a go-getter, you should attend a community meeting. However, many meetings are held at most 3-4 times yearly. If one of these meetings is coming up, ask if you can attend. Since you are not an owner, you will not be allowed to speak but have the right to listen to the meeting. If you have any concerns after attending, contact the management company or board of directors and request an appointment. If they are low on reserves or the financials do not look strong, ask them:

> ➢ What is the plan to increase the reserves?
> ➢ What is the plan to improve the financials and operating accounts?
> ➢ What are the significant issues facing the community?
> ➢ What is the participation level of the owners?

This is a significant investment, and the more due diligence you do, the more confident you can be of the purchase. You are responsible for investigating the property and the community, not your agent's, so take this job seriously.

How Can You Maximize Your Dues as a Current Owner?

Many owners only get involved with their community when they have a problem, or the dues increase. Many associations need help with owner apathy, and someone interested in serving as a director. But suppose you expect to experience a higher rate of return on your property because of the health of your association. In that case, you must be aware of the decisions being made on your board or better yet actively participate in board or committee meetings.

→ Know the Rules
There is no excuse to violate the rules if you know them. It is fruitless to ask for a repair not covered by your community in your CC&Rs. Remember to throw away your governing documents after you close escrow and plead ignorance. Familiarize yourself with these critical items once a year, particularly at the annual budget and election. Understand

the budget and the rationale for the changes made to it. Vote for qualified candidates, or run yourself if you have talents that would benefit the community. If you choose not to serve, interact with the board professionally and courteously. Lend your expertise to issues you can assist with and provide productive feedback to the board. If your community has committees, join the one where you can help most. If you decide to speak at board meetings, be informed and try to be positive.

→ The Squeaky Wheel Gets Oiled
Your board of directors are not mind readers. Owners often complain that an issue needs to be addressed with their property but fail to communicate it effectively with their board. If you have a problem, bring it up to your board appropriately. I recently had a concrete slab in the path to our front door rise and become a trip hazard. At our board meeting, I thanked the board for their service, acknowledged the hard work they were putting in on behalf of the community, and brought up the potential trip hazard in the common area of the concrete. The following day, there was a crew grinding down the concrete. If you speak up in a considerate but proper tone and request a repair, the association is legally obligated to address it; your board will respond appropriately almost every time. If you are a thorn in the board's side and complain about every issue but do not contribute to the success of your community, you may find they drag their collective feet.

→ Your Skills Are Needed
You may not be interested in serving on the board because you travel too much and cannot participate in meetings, or you do not have the time to do so; you may be able to contribute in other ways. In most associations, there needs to be more owner participation, and many hands make for lighter work. It takes several different skills to have a successful board, and you may have a skill they lack. Consider running for the board or volunteering for a committee, but at a minimum, participate actively in your board meetings and address issues facing your community. Lend your expertise to your board.

→ <u>Support the Board</u>

If your board must increase dues, levy a special assessment, or implement a new rule you have vetted and approved, stand up at a board meeting and state just that. I have witnessed board meetings when a few owners have spoken out angrily about the increase in dues, but when a respected owner spoke in support of the board and their decision, it changed the entire direction of the meeting. It is easy to attack the board because they made the decision, but it is harder to attack an owner who supports the board and the reasoning for their decision. I hope you agree that an increase in dues is not necessarily "bad" because that money is being used judiciously to increase reserves, pay for unexpected expenses, or in anticipation of imminent projects—hopefully, your board is being good stewards of the dues collected—and you can help educate other owners.

SECTION 3

THE BIG BAD BOARD OF DIRECTORS, aka THE SUPREME RULEMAKERS

"Stay committed to your decisions, but stay flexible in your approach".

TONY ROBBINS

The board of directors of a homeowners' Association is a body of elected or appointed members who equally oversee the activities of the Association. The board of directors, commonly called "the board," derives its powers, duties, and responsibilities from the Association's governing documents and, if applicable, state statutes.

These governing documents are generally the Association's by-laws and, in certain circumstances, the articles of incorporation and CC&Rs. The by-laws usually specify the number of board members, how the board members are to be chosen, and issues such as meeting requirements and other issues that deal with the operation of the Association. The board represents the association membership and is bound to act in every member's best interest.

Typically, most board members are elected at annual meetings by the association members; however, in certain situations, board members may be selected at a special membership meeting duly called for that purpose. Board members can also be appointed when associations are under developer control or when vacancies occur. Terms in office can vary from one Association's by-laws to another, and the number of board members can also differ drastically.

BEST PRACTICE #1 - Staggering Terms

Picture a board where all members are elected at once, yearly or every two years. It's like a rollercoaster of disruption and an orchestra without a conductor. This only invites chaos.

Our preferred and recommended method of board management is to staggard the board member terms. By staggering board positions, the community can ensure a steady flow of wisdom and guidance. Picture a board of three members, with one elected yearly for a three-year term. With having only one seat a year open, the other remaining board members have the wisdom and can help the new board member "learn the ropes". It's like passing the baton in a relay race.

The beauty of this approach is that the incoming board members can learn from the seasoned veterans, soaking up their wisdom like a sponge. With this transfer of knowledge, the harmony of governance is evident and keeps the drama minimized and keeps the pendulum from swinging wildly from one extreme to the other.

BEST PRACTICE #2 - Number of board members.

Finding the perfect recipe for harmony and productivity with the right mix of Board Members is crucial. Some communities might have grand ambitions, thinking that more is always better. They dream of having a board with a cast of characters that rivals a Broadway production - 5, 6, 7, or even ten board members! But let's pause and sprinkle a dash of wisdom on this idea.

In our world of HOAs, we've learned a thing or two about the magic number of board members. Firstly, odd is the way to go! Three, five, seven, or nine board members create the perfect balance and allow for that dramatic tie-breaking vote when needed.

Regarding the ideal number of board members, let's consider the size of the HOA. For those charming communities with fewer than 100 units, three (3) board members are ultra-efficient. However, for those larger communities with more than 150 members, a three-member board panel is still preferred, but if the community desires a little extra involvement, a five-member board might be the way to go.

We don't recommend more than five board members ever as we find that there are too many cooks in the kitchen, and the productivity and effectiveness of the board is minimized. You only have to look at local planning and zoning commissions or even the city council to see the wisdom in this approach.

It is also important to point out that the passage of time brings change. As an HOA matures and evolves, the challenge of finding willing volunteers can arise and having many board members makes this sometimes even more challenging.

Sometimes we get people saying but we want more people to be involved and our recommendation is that those people can serve on committees. There is no limit to the number of committees or the persons on those committees. Effectively utilizing committees is a way to balance needs over time without mandating it.

There is a difference between a director and an officer. In short, an individual is elected as a director to serve on the Association's board of directors, and then the directors convene among themselves to select the officers. The definition of an association director is an individual acting on behalf of the membership of an association. A director is responsible for overseeing the operation of the homeowners' Association and thus protecting the property values of the membership. Directors have the authority, as granted in the Association's governing documents and state statutes, if applicable, to hire and discharge vendors, call membership meetings, and determine other matters affecting the Association. The board of directors elects the officers. The Association's officers usually consist of a president, vice president, secretary, and treasurer. The officers have specific roles and duties regarding the operation of the Association, but their primary responsibility is the efficient operation of the Association.

Who Are the Officers?

❖ President

The ultimate goal of any board of directors is to increase the overall standard of living of the membership and the value of the property within the Association. The president is charged to lead this effort by doing the following:

→ Work closely with the other board members, association manager, and membership to determine the overall goals of the Association.
→ Have a good understanding of the Association's governing documents.
→ Be responsible for the Association's fiscal well-being. This includes collecting assessments, guiding the budget process, and ensuring that reserves are adequately funded.
→ Make Ensure adequate insurance coverage protects the Association from liability and other hazards.
→ Find and develop potential volunteers and future association leaders.
→ Maintain a close working relationship with the association manager and vendors to ensure the efficient operation of the Association.
→ Preside at board meetings and other association meetings. The president prepares meeting agendas and ensures that proper voting procedures are followed.
→ Effectively communicate with the membership, although being a great public speaker is unnecessary.
→ Enter into agreements with Management companies and Vendors.

❖ Vice President

The vice president is charged with all of the powers required to perform the duties of the association president in the absence of the president. The vice president needs to possess innate abilities or authority to act in the capacity of the association president. Generally, the vice president may only operate for the president when the president is physically absent or otherwise unable to perform. The vice president's duties are as follows:

→ Work closely with the president in establishing goals for the future.
→ Work closely with the president and provide needed input. In effect, the vice president acts as a sounding board for the president.

❖ **Secretary**

The duties of the secretary are as follows:

→ Record meeting minutes and board resolutions.
→ Affix the Association's corporate seal to legal documents and verify signatures on those documents.
→ Verify proxies for the Association's annual meeting and maintain and distribute all of the Association's records.
→ Take minutes.
→ Make resolutions on behalf of the board.
→ File the corporation with the secretary of state.

❖ **Treasurer**

As the name implies, the treasurer is the financial voice of the board and is charged with ensuring the Association's financial well-being. Generally, the treasurer is responsible for the Association's funds and keeping complete and accurate financial records. This does not mean the treasurer must perform accounting tasks but ensure they are being done. The duties of the treasurer are as follows:

→ Review the financials and take the lead on the annual budget.
→ Sign promissory notes of the Association.
→ Sign letters of engagement for audits.
→ Give the financial report at the annual meeting.
→ Make sure the federal and state tax returns are filed on time.
→ Recommend a reserve study firm.

Once a board is elected, the first step of an efficient operation is the establishment of clear, obtainable goals. Goal setting for a new board of directors creates a common purpose and objectives. These goals should have a limited number of objectives that the next annual membership meeting can accomplish.

Why Should You Run?

Some associations are on auto-drive, and being on the board requires little time and nominal effort. Other associations face major projects, weighty decisions on increases in dues or special assessments, and the time requirements are much higher. No matter which situation your Association faces, here are a few reasons to sacrifice some personal time and expertise for your Association:

❖ **Care About Your Community**

This is not only an association; it is your community and where you own a property. It may be where you live or own a rental, but I suspect it is one of your valuable assets. As the community goes, so does the value of that asset. It would help if you cared, and one way to protect that asset is to get involved with the body that makes financial and strategic decisions on behalf of that community.

I have a friend that once lived in a city and was oblivious to almost every aspect of that city. But once he was elected to the city council and nominated as mayor three times, he knew about every issue facing that city. If you would like to learn more about an organizations problems, then simply serve. The same holds for an association board. You will understand every facet of your community by serving on the board of directors.

❖ **Broken Windows**

There is a theory about a broken window on an abandoned

house: it attracts more crime and additional broken windows. It appears to those who mean no good that no one cares about the property, and it offers the least resistance. The same holds for associations. If owners allow their dogs to poop all over the place, or the landscapers do a haphazard job, or rules are not enforced, it appears to owners that the board does not care. The council may be paying a management company that does not care, but the owners will hold the board accountable for not having the management company responsible. Do not let your community suffer from broken windows.

❖ No One Else

Sadly, many associations need help to get owner participation on the board. In small associations or communities with many rentals where the owners live elsewhere, associations need help with owner apathy. It may be time for you to step up when no one else will.

❖ Self-Serving

Being a part of the board could actually play to your properties advantage and help get things moving on your own terms. It might sound a bit paradoxical, but being an active member of the board can be a bit of a self-serving gig, especially if you want to see property values go up or prevent that special person from making life more difficult.

What Are the Cons of Being on a Board?

If it were all rainbows and unicorns, running for a board position would be like running for the city council, but rarely are there twenty owners running for three board positions in a hundred-owner association. There must be something more than time constraints holding the owners back from serving. What are the cons?

❖ Bad Cop

Boards hold owners accountable and enforce the rules. If

board members themselves become the HOA Police, the owner whose car is towed may find it hard to forget this decision and hold a grudge against their neighbor. Making tough decisions comes with the territory, and some owners resent those decisions. Many boards hire a management company to do the uncomfortable and less glamorous tasks, such as enforcing rules to minimize situations like these.

❖ Wrath of Raising Dues

Owners may need to know what happens at the Association, but they notice when the monthly dues increase. Even if the increase is due to inflation, which is entirely reasonable and justifiable, some owners will squawk regardless. It may not matter how much you explain or communicate; any increase will be intolerable.

❖ Collections and Foreclosures

There may come a time when an owner refuses to pay their assessments, and they receive a pre-lien letter, a lien, a collection, and one day, you may have to authorize a foreclosure of their property to recover the dues owed to the Association. The very worst outcome is possibly, the owners may be evicted from the property, losing this asset because the board enforced their powers. It may be challenging, but it is correct, and the board has a fiduciary duty to the Association to follow through and apply equal enforcement to everyone.

❖ Monthly Meetings

If the president does not control the meeting, meetings can last longer than necessary and consume a few hours of your evening once a month. Using Robert's Rules to maintain order is essential.

What are Robert's Rules? *Robert's Rules of Order* is a book on parliamentary procedure that is still considered the standard for running an efficient and fair meeting. Brigadier General Henry M. Robert graduated from the United States Military Academy in 1857 and received a commission in the Army. He was once asked to chair a church meeting and became embarrassed because of his lack of knowledge regarding parliamentary procedures. At the time, various forms of parliamentary procedures were being followed, so he published a standardized manual that eventually became *Robert's Rules of Order*, issued in 1876. The critical points of Robert's Rules are as follows:

- **Meeting Structure:** The book outlines the typical structure of a meeting, from calling the meeting to order to adjourning it.
- **Agenda:** Meetings should follow a set agenda to address various topics in an organized manner.
- **Presiding Officer:** The chairperson or presiding officer is responsible for maintaining order, recognizing speakers, and ensuring that discussions adhere to the rules.
- **Motions:** Members can make motions to propose actions or decisions, and these motions need to be seconded and then discussed before being put to a vote.
- **Debate:** Members can discuss the pros and cons of a motion in a structured manner, with the presiding officer controlling the speaking time and ensuring civility.
- **Amendments:** Motions can be modified or amended through a specific process.
- **Voting:** Members vote on motions using various methods, including voice votes, show of hands, or ballots. There are also rules for counting votes and resolving tie votes.
- **Order of Precedence:** Certain motions take precedence over others, and the rules provide guidance on the order in which different motions should be considered.
- **Committees:** The rules explain how committees can be formed, their functions, and how they report back to the main assembly.
- **Point of Order:** Members can raise a point of order if they believe the rules are being violated during a meeting.
- **Appeals:** Members can appeal the decision of the chairperson if they believe a ruling was incorrect.
- **Quorum:** The minimum number of members required to conduct business must be present for decisions to be valid.

❖ The Nitty-Gritty of Meetings

Agenda: At least several days before the meeting, an agenda must be prepared, posted for the members, and distributed to the board. Supporting documentation as it relates to the items on the agenda, such as the treasurer's report, manager's report, minutes from the previous meeting, and other documents, should be included in a board packet. The board packet should lay out the details and create the groundwork for the issues at hand to be discussed. An organized and timed agenda allows the board to work much more efficiently. A strictly timed agenda keeps discussion of issues and actions moving efficiently. The agenda should do the following:

→ Set a time limit for the meeting length and discussion of each agenda item.
→ Include a descriptive sentence on topics to clarify issues. An action statement of the needed motion helps identify what is required to move the issue along (e.g., "We have been asked to allow grills on the clubhouse patio, but the association manager recommends that we not approve because of fire hazard concerns."
→ Prepare motions before the meeting. The president should state the motions on the agenda that are expected to be made.
→ List new business on the agenda. Strive to eliminate surprises at the board meeting; no decisions should be made on issues not presented on the agenda beforehand. The members have a right to address anything that impacts their ownership.
→ List any action delayed by the board from a prior board meeting as an agenda item to be reported or acted on.

A board member packet should include:
- Agenda
- Minutes to be approved from the prior meeting
- Financials
- Membership delinquency report
- Invoice copies

- Maintenance proposals
- New business
- Warning letters
- Member correspondence with the board.

Minutes: An association's meeting minutes are the written legal record of the board's meetings. The board secretary is responsible for compiling and, once approved, maintaining these records in the Association's files. Minutes are so vital that they will be held indefinitely in the Association's records. Board members come and go, but the minutes are permanent.

Minutes are used to document decisions made during a meeting and also provide a description of actions taken. Minutes are not word-for-word transcripts of everything that was said, but instead, they reflect what was accomplished at the meeting. Generally, a meeting's business should fit on one page or at least two. Minutes must be taken for all board and annual meetings, committee meetings, and any special board or membership meetings. CC&R violation hearings must be documented in the minutes. The primary content of the meeting minutes is as follows:
- Association name
- Specific meeting type (board, annual, etc.)
- Date
- Location of meeting (legal address)
- Time meeting called to order
- Name of board or committee members in attendance
- Statement that quorum was established
- Precise wording of every adopted motion
- Notations of failed or withdrawn motions
- Name of the person who made the motion
- Name of the person who seconded the motion
- Names of those dissenting if a vote was not unanimous
- Committee reports given or submitted
- Member's name and discussion topic, if the membership is allowed to address the board.
- Items that will be discussed at future meetings
- Date, time, and location of the next meeting, if determined
- Time of adjournment
- Signatures of the secretary and president/meeting chair

and dates once minutes are approved

Meeting minutes provide a historical and legal record of the operations of the Association. Matters dealing with personal issues and opinions that have no bearing on the association's business should never be noted in the Association's minutes. Minutes are subject to review and legal discovery in membership and non-membership lawsuits. This means **meeting minutes should be precise and brief, and they should not be subjective**. Minutes should be clear and concise, with only a basic summary of the business conducted, debated, and voted upon.

Motions: All motions must be seconded and are adopted by the majority vote unless otherwise noted. All activities must be debated unless otherwise noted. Signs are in order of precedence: motions may be made only if no equal or higher priority motion is on the floor. When a signal is made and seconded, directors may speak to the action, debate the move, and vote to approve or deny the motion.

→ **Make a motion:** To introduce a new piece of business or propose a decision or an action, a motion must be made by a group member ("I move that . . ."). A second motion must also be made (Raise your hand and say, "I second it."). After limited discussion, the group then votes on the motion. For the motion to pass, a majority vote (or quorum as specified in your by-laws) is required.

→ **Postpone an item indefinitely:** This tactic kills a motion. Once passed, the action cannot be reintroduced at that meeting; it may be brought up again later. A sign is made ("I move to postpone indefinitely . . ."), a second is required, and a majority vote is necessary to postpone the motion under consideration.

→ **Amend a motion:** This process changes a motion under consideration. Perhaps you like the idea proposed, but not exactly as offered. Raise your hand and make the following: "I move to amend the motion on the floor." This also requires a second. After the motion to amend is seconded, a majority vote is needed to determine whether the amendment is accepted. Then, a vote is taken on the amended action. In some organizations, a "friendly amendment" is made. If the person who made the original motion agrees with the suggested changes, the amended motion may be voted on without a separate vote to approve the amendment.

→ **Commit a motion:** Imagine you're putting a tag on a motion, like a "to-do" label. This step needs someone to second it, showing that more than one person agrees it's worth considering. Then, when the group votes on it, most of them need to say "yes" for it to move forward. At the next meeting, the group in charge of the motion, which we'll call the committee, has to create a report about what the motion is all about. If there's already a committee that fits the bill, the motion heads over to them. But if there isn't a suitable committee, a brand new one is formed to handle it. It's like giving a motion its own special team to figure things out.

→ **Call for the question:** To end a debate immediately, the question is called (say, "I call for the question,") and the action needs a second. A vote is held directly (no further questioning is allowed). A two-thirds vote is required for passage. If it is passed, the motion on the floor is voted on immediately.

→ **Table a discussion:** To table a debate is to lay aside the business at hand in such a manner that it will be considered later in the meeting or at another time ("I make a motion to table this discussion until the next meeting. In the meantime, we will get more information so we can better discuss the issue.") A second is needed and a majority vote required to table the item under discussion.

→ **Adjourn a meeting:** A motion is made to end the session. A second motion is required. A majority vote is then required for the meeting to adjourn (completed).

Here are the other motions in order of precedence:
- Motion to adjourn: Not debatable. Goes to an immediate majority vote.
- Motion to recess: Not debatable. Maybe for a specific time.
- Motion to appeal the chair's decision: Not debatable. Goes

to immediate vote. Allows the body to overrule a decision made by the chair.

- Motion to suspend the rules: Suspends formal process for dealing with a specific issue. Debatable. Requires a two-thirds vote.
- Motion to end debate and vote or move the main question ("Call the question"): Applies only to the motion on the floor. Not debatable. Requires a two-thirds vote.
- Motion to extend debate: This can be general or for a specific time or number of speakers. Refers questions to a specific group with a specific time and charge.
- Motion to refer to committee: Applies only to the main motion. Refers to questions to a specific group with a specific time and cost.

SECTION 4

GOVERNING DOCUMENTS

"No man is good enough to govern another man without that other man's consent".

Abraham Lincoln

There is a hierarchy of authority when it comes to the governing documents of a HOA:

→ **Federal law** supersedes all: The laws adopted by the federal government take precedence over everything else. Unless the Supreme Court determines a law is unconstitutional, it becomes the law of the land.

→ **State laws**: The state can pass laws more restrictive than federal law. For example, there are seven protected classes at the federal level but seventeen at the state level.

→ **City laws**: A city may pass laws more restrictive than state or federal laws. A good example is rent control. Although the state recently passed rent control for specific properties and limited rent increases to 5 percent over the consumer price index, a city may limit rent increases by a lower amount and offer higher relocation fees to tenants.

→ **Declaration of CC&Rs**: These are recorded when the association is formed and set out the community's ownership conditions. It is tough to change the CC&Rs; often, ten have never been changed by an association.

→ **Bylaws**: The bylaws detail the organizational structure of the HOA, including the roles of board members, meetings, voting procedures, and more

→ **Articles of incorporation**: The "birth certificate" of the association is the legal document required to create a non-profit status corporation. Bylaws: These serve as the roadmap to the association's day-to-day operations.

→ **Operating rules**: The community's rules can be easily modified and changed to suit the association's needs.

→ **Architectural Rules**: Many HOA's have architectural or design guidelines that dictate the appearance of homes and improvements withing the community. These may cover elements such as exterior paint colors, landscaping, fencing and other aesthetic considerations.

→ **Resolutions and Policies:** HOAs might adopt resolutions and policies to address specific issues that arise over time. These could include policies on trash disposal, pool usage and other matters not covered in the CC&R or bylaws or even a rule.

It's important to note that the hierarchy is structured in a way that ensures higher-level documents take precedence over lower-level ones. If there's a conflict between documents, the more specific and restrictive rule usually prevails. Additionally, any changes to the governing documents typically require a formal process, often involving homeowner approval.

Understanding this hierarchy helps residents and board members navigate the rules and regulations of the HOA community, ensuring a well-organized and harmonious living environment.

Formation Documents
- Declarations of annexation (or supplementary CC&Rs) used in multi-phased developments
- Condominium plans (when applicable) and subdivision maps
- Conditional use permits
- HUD regulatory agreements
- Utility or maintenance easements or deeds

Covenants, Conditions, and Restrictions, aka CC&Rs: This declaration is recorded with the county recorder's office and is reflected in the actual title to all real property within the HOA. The statement sets out conditions that every owner must comply with as an association member. The covenants in a HOA are specifically designed to maintain and preserve the actual property values within the development.

CC&Rs typically describe the prohibited use of the property within the development and allocate responsibility for the required maintenance of the separate interests and common areas. The declaration is a property use document that describes the development and ownership interests of the association and the individual owners; sets forth the covenants governing the use, operation, and obligations relative to ownership of a separate interest; and sets up the association's ability to assess the individual interest owners.

Equitable servitude: This is a legal concept that describes a promise running successively from one landowner to another as title to the property is exchanged from time to time. In essence, CC&Rs are promises made between neighbors. It is also referred to as a "covenant running with the land" or "covenant," as in the expanded title of the governing document, declaration of covenants, conditions, and restrictions. These promises are memorialized by recording them in the title to the property. For example, a typical covenant includes requirements for the owners to pay assessments and the association to obtain insurance.

All owners of separate interests in an HOA benefit from and are bound by the declaration's covenants (equitable servitudes) and restrictions. The order's contents are enforceable unless they are against public policy, unreasonable, or enforced arbitrarily or capriciously. Any separate interest owner, the association, or both may execute most servitudes. Typically, the association enforces the declaration (e.g., assessment obligations).

Amending the CC&Rs: Amendments and changes to the declaration are made under the procedures outlined in the governing documents. For an amendment to be enforceable, all of the following steps must occur:
- → Property Notice to all members of the proposed changes in the governing documents.
- → A meeting to vote or a mail-in ballot can be created to adopt the new governing document(s) or amendment(s).
- → The HOA/COA cannot require more than a supermajority (67%) vote of the unit owners to amend the governing documents. Also, the association cannot require any specific member to approve an amendment to those documents. Utah Code §§ 57-8a-104, 57-8a-104, 57-8-39. However, the CC&R and bylaws may lower the threshold lower than a supermajority to even a simple majority of the membership.
- → Once approved, the document is prepared and recorded at the county level.
- → Supermajority requirements are typically found in CC&Rs older than ten years old. Many HOAs modify those to mean a majority because it takes time to get members to respond.

4. Enforcement of the CC&Rs: Effective enforcement begins with good planning and governing documents that are clear, fair, and reasonable and that "due process" is offered in their enforcement. The association may not have unreasonable restrictions, and all rules must be reasonable. Utah Code §§ 57-8a-218(14), 57-8-8.1(6). Some common rules and restrictions are:

→ Construction and alterations
→ Smoking restrictions
→ Architectural control procedures
→ Pet, parking, and vehicle limits
→ Rental restrictions

In Utah, every association should have a Fine and Hearing Policy outlining the steps taken and fines levied. Owners in a COA may not be charged a fee greater than $500 a month in aggregate penalties for violations of the same rule or provision of the governing documents. Utah Code § 57-8-37 while Owners in an HOA have no limit.

How Is Conflict Between Owners and the Board Mitigated?

Disputes sometimes arise between unit owners and association management over whether a fine should be assessed for an alleged violation of the association's rules or provisions. State law in Utah Code §§ 57-8a-208 (HOAs) and 57-8-37 (COAs) provide rights to unit owners. A summary of these rights is below:

HOAs must provide a warning before assessing fines. The notice must:
1. Describe the violation;
2. State the rule the owner is alleged to have violated;
3. Provide a notice that a fine may be imposed if a violation is not cured or if another violation of the same provision occurs within the next year; and
4. Provide a time frame (not less than 48 hours) to cure a violation if the violation is continuous.

The Utah Law provides a clear framework for resolving disputes within an association and among its members. However, suppose a unit owner has already been warned of a violation within the past year or fails to fix a continuous violation. In that case, no further warning is necessary before the HOA/COA can take action on that rule or provision. Utah Code §§ 57-8a-208(2)(b-c), 57-8-37(2)(b-c).

If a fine is assessed against a unit owner, the owner has 30 days from the notice of assessment to appeal through an informal hearing before the HOA's/COA's board or committee. At the hearing, the unit owner must be given a reasonable opportunity to present the owner's position and allowed participation by electronic transmission if desired. While this hearing is pending, the HOA cannot assess interest or late fees against the owner for not paying the set fine.

If the HOA upholds the decision to assess the fine at the hearing, or if the unit owner chooses not to request a hearing, the penalty assessed may be appealed to state court by initiating a civil action. This civil action must be filed within 180 days from:

1. The day the owner receives a final decision from the board if an informal hearing was requested or;
2. The day the 30 days to request an informal hearing passes, if no informal hearing was requested.

❖ Articles of Incorporation

The articles of incorporation set forth the association's purpose and serve as the "birth certificate" of the corporate entity. They are filed with the secretary of state's office when the HOA is incorporated. The articles of incorporation typically include the initial board of directors and fiscal year-end. Bylaws are corporate documents that usually are neither filed nor recorded but are kept with the official books and records of the association. Bylaws govern the association's day-to-day operations.

❖ Operating Rules

An operating rule is a regulation adopted by the board of directors "that generally applies to the management and operation of the common interest development or the conduct of the business and affairs of the association." For an operating rule to be valid and enforceable, it must be:
- Reasonable
- In writing
- Within the authority of the board of directors to enact
- Consistent with the governing laws and the CC&Rs, articles of incorporation, and by-laws
- Adopted, amended, or repealed in good faith and compliance with the requirements of law.

The procedure for adoption is as follows:
- For HOAs, at least 15 Days before making the rule change, the board of directors provides the membership with a written notice of a proposed rule change (The notice must include the text of the proposed change, its effect, and a description of the purpose behind the change.) as well as a time for a meeting to discuss the proposed rule changes. For COAs, no notice is required.
- After the board considers any comments by the membership, the rule change is adopted, as stated, at a board of directors meeting.
- Following the adoption of the rule changes, the board notices the change(s) to every member.

Members who disagree on a rule change may call for a special meeting within 60 days from the rule's adoption date. If 51% of the total votes in the association vote to disapprove of the government at the special meeting, then power will be nullified. The procedure for lot owners to call a special session is usually outlined in laws or CC&Rs.

In 2023 – the PUD Act, SB191, clarifies what constitutes a "rule" in an HOA/COA setting. Under SB191, a Rule is a "policy, guideline, restriction, procedure, or regulation...that is not outlined in a contract, easement, article of incorporation or bylaw, or declaration" that "governs the conduct of persons or the use, quality, type, design, or appearance of real property or personal property."

Internal business operating procedures of a board are NOT considered rules under SB191.

Additionally, any legal action to challenge a PUD HOA's adoption of any rules must be commenced within 18 months after the board took the action being challenged in the law-making process under UCA §57-8a-217. In other words, the legislature created a statute of limitations of 18 months to dispute the adoption of a law in an HOA setting.

Emergencies allow exception to rule adoption procedures: Notice is not required if the board of directors determines an immediate rule change is necessary to address either of the following risks:
- Imminent threat to public health or safety
- Imminent risk of substantial economic loss to the association

If the board determines an immediate rule change is necessary, it can adopt an "emergency rule change" effective for 120 days (or less if specified in the rule change). An emergency rule change may be readopted only according to standard (non-emergency) adoption procedures.

Rule Changes: Generally, it is within the board's authority to institute rule changes unless the CC&Rs require membership approval for rules. There may also be cases when a law requires a rule change. Issuing a document that merely repeats the existing law or the governing documents is not a "rule change." The following actions by the board of directors of an association also are not rule changes:
- A decision regarding the maintenance of the common area
- A decision on a specific matter that is not intended to apply generally
- A decision setting the amount of a regular or special assessment

How Can You Change the Rules (And Keep the Peace)?

One of the most essential duties of the board and the management company is to enforce the community rules. Rules apply to owners who live in the community and renters who occupy the property. The enforcement of regulations is the most tangible evidence that living in an association is very different from living in a property that is not an HOA because everyone is held accountable for their behavior to the same set of rules. The board has the power to modify those rules without a vote of the members. How do you change your practices without antagonizing your members? Here are a few pointers:

❖ Make Them Reasonable

Utah law dictates that association rules must be reasonable and lawful. The board must institute a new government by federal and state law. A commission cannot ban all pets because comfort animals are protected by fair housing, and the courts have already ruled that anyone should be entitled to at least one pet. But it is reasonable that the owner of a pet must clean up after their animal, and if they do not, they can be fined.

❖ Obtain Buy-In

The community should vet any rule. If most owners want to be able to park in the streets at night, rather than banning all parking on the roads, the board may consider putting time limits on parking in community areas. This stops residents from using community areas for their permanent personal use but allows this space to be used by all. Imposing a rule that the majority of the community does not want will only result in severe backlash to the board. But if 80 percent of the community is for a rule change, the remaining 20 percent may not like it but must abide by it.

❖ Give Proper Notice

Over-communicate a change in your rules and give the community ample notice. The law says if you are an HOA, you must provide fifteen days of information before implementing a rule change, but the board should give much more time to effect the change: at least forty days. Once the rule is in effect, the board may want to have a grace period, where rather than fining the transgressor, the board issues a warning. As every board knows, many owners ignore the board's actions (unless you raise the dues), so a gentle transition to a new rule, mainly if a monetary fine is included or if a vehicle is to be towed for violating that rule, is recommended.

❖ Abide by Them

Once you make a rule change, enforce them. Many associations have rules that are not enforced or are enforced intermittently. If you have hired a management company, this is a crucial role they play for you: bad cop. The enforcer should be someone other than board members that implement fining residents and noting violations as it will not create a pleasant relationship with your members. Let the management company report the violations, levy the fines, and set up the process to tow cars. If the rules are uniformly enforced, members will take notice and commit to the new regulations. Work with a management company with the expertise and ability to assist you in the complexities of leading your community.

❖ Common Areas

A common area is everything within the HOA except the separate interest and may consist of mutual or reciprocal easement rights. Exclusive-use common area is a portion of the common area used by one or more, but not all, separate interest owners. Below are some examples that may include:
- Patios and balconies
- Carports and garages
- Telephone wiring serving units

Separate interest is that an individual owner in an HOA owns

uniquely from any other owner. Here are a few examples:
- Community: the exclusive right to occupy an apartment
- Planned development: separately owned lot, parcel, area, or space
- Stock cooperative: the exclusive right to occupy a portion of real property
- Condominium project: individual unit as defined by final recorded map, parcel map, or condominium plan

The main difference between HOAs and COAs is that with an HOA, all owners commonly own the common area. In contrast, in a COA, each owner owns a percentage of the common area and has the right to sell their ownership interest as if they were selling a separately owned property.

What Happens When an Owner Sells?

When an owner sells, there is a transfer of ownership interest, and an association member transfers the ownership rights of the separate interest, membership in the association, and any additional ownership rights granted (e.g., an undivided interest in the common area, easements, right to use amenities). Even if a buyer agrees, the seller cannot retain use privileges for standard area amenities (e.g., swimming pool, golf course, tennis court, clubhouse).

❖ Set Up or Transfer Fees

The management company charges an HOA setup or transfer fee to provide a demand to escrow, ensure all previous owner debts are paid at the close of escrow, and provide documentation to the buyer through escrow for review and approval. Typical documentation provided is as follows:
- CC&Rs
- Budget
- Reserve studies
- Minutes
- Rules and regulations
- Annual budget

The management company puts the new owner's name in the management software and provides fobs, keys, and association access to the new owner.

❖ Reinvestment Fees

Under Utah law, community associations can impose a closing fee on property sales up to a maximum of 0.5% of the sale price. However, this provision does not apply to communities with over 500 units or 500 acres. There are very few of those in Utah.

Like other closing costs, such as those related to real estate commissions title insurance, the HOA reinvestment fee can be paid upfront by the buyer or seller or included in the loan through seller concessions.

The HOA reinvestment fee is specifically designated for the community association and cannot be passed on to other parties or used for external projects. The association must utilize all funds collected through this fee for community reinvestment purposes, including maintaining, upkeep, and improving common areas that benefit association members. This money doesn't go to management companies or developers and stays part of the association.

It's important to note that the reinvestment fee only applies when a home is sold and does not come into effect during all title transfers. For instance, if a property is transferred due to the homeowner's death to their heirs, moved to a close family member, ordered by a court, or involves any other involuntary transfer, the reinvestment fee does not apply.

One significant advantage of the HOA reinvestment fee is its contribution to keeping monthly assessments low. When a home sells for $500,000 in an HOA with a 0.5% reinvestment fee, the association will receive $2,500. This additional income can be reinvested in the community, reducing the reliance on assessment funds and helping to maintain lower assessments for all residents. Over the average duration of homeownership in Utah, around 8-12 years, the reinvestment fee can yield substantial returns for homeowners.

However, one drawback of the HOA reinvestment fee is that it may come as an unexpected expense for home buyers, adding to the stress of the closing process.

SECTION 5

BEST PRACTICES

"Coming together is a beginning; keeping together is progress; working together is success."

HENRY FORD

Some states have recognized that the Declaration of CC&Rs is the constitution of the HOA and is legally binding upon residents to the extent that it does not conflict with state or federal law. CC&Rs, once adequately recorded, are presumed valid until proven otherwise. Courts have explained the quasi-governmental nature of the HOA: the homeowners' association functions almost "as a second municipal government, regulating many aspects of [the homeowners'] daily lives.

Upon analysis of the association's functions, one sees the association as a quasi-government entity paralleling, in almost every case, a municipal government's powers, duties, and responsibilities. As a 'mini government,' the association provides to its members, in almost every case, utility services, road maintenance, street and common area lighting, and refuse removal.

In many cases, it also provides security services and various forms of communication within the community. There is, moreover, a clear analogy to the municipal police and public safety functions." In short, homeowner's associations, via their enforcement of the CC&Rs, provide many beneficial and desirable services that permit an HOA to flourish.

❖ The Big Bad Board of Directors

Being on a board of directors means you must follow a codified standard of conduct and subject you to specific laws and requirements. A director must perform their duties in good faith, in a manner such a director believes to be in the corporation's best interests, and with such care, including reasonable inquiry, as an ordinarily prudent person would use under similar circumstances. A director's responsibility is to take any sensible action within its stated powers, provided laws or governing documents do not restrict such activities. On the other hand, individual directors have greater exposure to risk for themselves and the association. Board members of HOAs, whether owners or developers are responsible for the money and property of others. They are, therefore, in a "fiduciary capacity" with a duty to act for the benefit of those "others" and not for themselves.

❖ Indemnification of Board or Agent

A corporation would have the power to protect its agent (i.e., director, employee, management firm) against judgments, fines, and defense costs in connection with any legal proceeding "if such person acted in good faith and in a manner such person reasonably believed to be in the best interests of the corporation." In criminal proceedings, the corporation's agent must have had no reasonable cause to believe the conduct was unlawful. Unless the governing documents impose more stringent standards, the board shall do the following tasks on at least a monthly basis:

- Review a current reconciliation of the association's operating accounts.
- Review a current reconciliation of the association's reserve accounts.
- Review the current year's actual reserve revenues and expenses compared to the current year's budget.
- Review the income and expense statement for the association's operating and reserve accounts.
- Review the latest account statements prepared by the financial institutions where the association has operating and reserve accounts.
- Prepare an account for litigation expenses unless the governing documents impose more stringent standards.

The fiduciary responsibility of the board of directors is to protect the assets of the association by ensuring:

- A preventative maintenance program to protect the physical assets in the common area
- Adequate reserve funding to prepare for the replacement and significant repair of common area components
- Safe investment of association funds to protect the principal
- Established checks and balances in the day-to-day handling of association funds to protect them from improper use
- Proper internal financial controls and risk management
- Adequate insurance coverage by the association.

❖ The Financials

Like banks use financial reports to gauge a business's economic health, the non-profit association's financial statements reflect its current and future economic health. Most directors are not well versed in "financials," it is critical for all board members, not just the treasurer, to grasp the basics of accounting and the financial reports they are reviewing.

There are three main methods of accounting: cash, accrual, and modified accrual basis (sometimes called modified cash basis). The basis of accounting indicates the way transactions are posted and reported. Here are the differences:

- Cash: income is reported only when the money is received, and expenses are reported only when invoices are paid.
- Accrual: income reported when earned, not necessarily when received, and expenses reported when incurred but not necessarily when they are paid.
- Modified accrual: income reported when earned, not when received, and expenses reported when paid like cash.

Most households and businesses use the cash basis for their financial reports. That makes sense because it reflects the "true" cash position of the entity. But how the books are kept for homeowners' associations is different. The former operating budget must be created annually and not on a cash basis. Why do they do it this way?

Because owners are legally obligated to pay their dues and risk a collection or even foreclosure, the association will eventually realize the income from every owner. They can expect the payment rather than "guess" at the expected revenue when creating an annual budget. On the expense side, using the accrual method, contracts that the association has committed to, such as insurance, landscaping, and utilities, are automatically expensed monthly. There may be funds in the bank, but they will have been accounted for already in the accrual method and will not be available to spend. Some boards budget using the accrual method but use the cash basis for monthly financials to get both a macro and micro view of their financial position.

❖ Reports

A few reports are delivered monthly to the board or the treasurer, depending on the board's will. If a board meets quarterly, the treasurer may review the financials in the off months. Here are the reports my company, Maxfield Community Management, provides to its board every month:

- **Cash Flow Statement** - The Cash Flow report is a commonly used report that shows the net change in G.L. account balances over a specified date range and includes the **Net Operating Income** total for that date range.
- **Balance Sheet** - The report shows balances of assets, liabilities, and capital for a property or group of properties on the day it is run. This helps owners see the liquidated value for all of their cash (bank accounts) and assets and determine how much of that is theirs to keep (capital) and how much of this is owed (liability).
- **Income Statement** - The Income Statement (**often called a P&L**) allows an owner to see their gross income, gross expense, and net operating income (income minus expenses) for one calendar month. It also includes fiscal year-to-date totals to preview these totals for the fiscal (tax) year.
- **Bank Account Activity** - The Bank Account Activity report is intended to provide a running balance and total available funds in a specific bank account by showing all transactions tied to that account.
- **Bank Reconciliation Report** - This report reconciles the general ledger and must equal $0. Maxfield uses Triple Tie Out Trust accounting methods, which ensures that every debit and credit has been accounted for.
- **Homeowner Delinquency Balance** - This is a list of homeowners currently delinquent in paying their monthly dues.
- **Homeowner Prepayment Balance** - This shows who

has paid ahead, which is a liability to the Association until earned.

- **Homeowner Directory -** This report shows the contact information for the association members. This report should not be shared with the homeowners as it contains private information that the board can have.
- **Violation Detail Report -** This report lists all the outstanding violations in the community.
- **Budget comparison (budget to actual) -** This compares the month and the annual income and expenditures to what the community expected to collect and spend.
- General ledger summary: This report reflects every payment made to every vendor for the month.
- Accounts payable check register: The association pays Every check, and the check number is shown in this report. This is a quick way to check that the management company is not writing checks to non-authorized companies.
- Bank reconciliation: This reconciles the general ledger and must equal $0 to reflect that every debit and credit has been accounted for.
- Copies of Paid Work Orders and Bills - these copies are attached to the report.

❖ **Annual Calendar**

Every year, the board must approve and authorize certain activities, some mandated by law and others just good business operating practices. Here are activities most associations include on their calendar:

- Registering the corporation with the secretary of state (every two years)
- Annual elections
- Annual pro-forma operating budget
- Reserve study (on site every six years, desk review in off years)
- Tax returns for the previous tax year
- Review of the annual financial statement using the accrual basis of accounting by a C.P.A. if the association's gross income exceeds $150,000 (includes

an audit of the management company)
- Vendor review (includes a review of insurance requirements)
- Distribution of a copy of the annual review to members within 30 days of the calendar or fiscal year-end

❖ Required Disclosures

Utah statutes require the board to provide and make available certain financial information to association members. Mailing of documents and disclosures usually becomes the responsibility of the community manager.

❖ Anticipated Assessment

Any increase in regular assessments must be provided by individual notice to the owners between thirty and sixty days before the growth becomes due. Notice requirements for special assessments are the same as increases in regular inspections unless the particular review is for an extraordinary expense. In emergencies, a written finding of the necessity for the special assessment must be included in the "Notice of the Special Assessment."

❖ Annual Budget Report Alternative

Instead of the annual budget report, a summary of the yearly budget report may be distributed with a written notice that the complete information is available to any member upon request and includes instructions on requesting a copy.

❖ Availability of Minutes

Minutes often contain significant financial information and, as such, are required to be made available to members. The minutes of board meetings should reflect that Utah code requirements completed the annual mailing of financial disclosure documents.

❖ Insurance Coverage

The association must distribute a summary of the association's property, general liability, earthquake (if included), flood (if required), and fidelity insurance policies, including the insurer's name, type of insurance, policy limits, and amount of deductibles. Members must be notified of the following by individual delivery as soon as practical after renewal, cancellation, or change in coverage: termination, coverage lapse, non-renewal, or significant changes in scope or deductible.

❖ Penalties and Fines, aka Fine and Hearing Policy

An association may adopt a policy imposing monetary penalties or fees on association members, provided the authority exists in the declaration before its adoption. If such a policy is in place, a schedule of the monetary penalties that may be assessed must be distributed to each member. Policy disclosure must be via individual delivery. Penalties may be imposed for violations of the governing documents or rules of the association and may relate to the activities of a member's guest, invitee, or tenant.

❖ Owner Notice Disclosure

Utah law requires that an owner be requested to provide the best contact information so the board can provide accurate delivery of disclosures and billing information. This contact information should include the owner's name, address, and phone number. If the property is rented, it may also require the knowledge of the tenant.

❖ Member Inspection Rights

Community associations must make the books and records available and open to inspection by all members for purposes reasonably related to that members' interest within the association. In 2023, SB191 further clarifies what constitutes an official record that an HOA or COA. must provide to its members upon request. These records include a copy of the HOA/COA's:
1. Governing documents
2. Most recent approved meeting minutes

3. most recent budget and financial statement
4. most recent reserve analysis and
5. The certificate of insurance for each HOA/COA policy
6. The first three documents listed above should be maintained on the website of the HOA/COA if the HOA/COA has an official website. Otherwise, the papers should be made readily available at the office of the HOA/COA.

An HOA/COA should also maintain the following records at its "principal office" and make them available for owners to copy or inspect:
1. Minutes of all member meetings during the last three years
2. Records of all actions taken by members without an appointment during the last three years
3. All written communications sent to members generally for the previous three years
4. A list of all the names and business or home addresses of the current directors and officers
5. A copy of the most recent annual report delivered to the Utah Department of Commerce
6. Division of Corporations and Commercial Code (yearly renewal)
7. All financial statements the HOA/COA has prepared during the last three years that a member can request.

The following documents need to be kept as permanent records of the HOA/COA and provided to a requesting member upon written demand and a showing that the request for the form (s) is in good faith and for a proper purpose.
1. Minutes of all meetings of its members and directors
2. Record of all actions taken by the members of the board without a meeting
3. Record of all actions taken by an HOA/COA committee on behalf of the HOA/COA;
4. Record all waivers of notices of member and board meetings or any committee meetings.
5. Record of HOA/COA members - names and addresses, in alphabetical order, showing the number of votes

they are entitled to exercise.

6. Other applicable Nonprofit Act record request sections include U.C.A. §16-6a-1602, 1603, 1605, 1606, and 1610.

SB191 specifically provides that the following items are NOT an official HOA/COA record that must be provided to owners upon request: "correspondence, communications, notes, or other similar information, regardless of format or method of storage, that is not an official decision, published document, or record of the corporation."

The preceding is a summary of the recordkeeping responsibilities of an HOA/COA and should not be relied upon for legal purposes. Please get in touch with your legal counsel for more specific information and details. There are still statutory penalties for an HOA/COA who fails to comply with a records request.

❖ **Information That Can Be Withheld or Redacted**

According to the civil code, the association has the right to withhold or delete the following information:

- Information privileged under law
- Information "reasonably likely to lead to identity theft"
- Information reasonably likely to lead to fraud in connection with the association
- Information reasonably likely to compromise the privacy of a member
- Information contains records of disciplinary actions, collection activities, payment plans, personnel records (other than certain payroll records), executive session agendas or minutes, or interior architectural plans

❖ **Place of Inspection**

The law requires the association to make its records available for inspection and copying at its business office within the HOA Suppose the association does not have a business office within the development. In that case, the documents must be available for inspection and copying at a place agreed upon by the requesting member and association. It is also reasonable and allowed under Utah law that a reasonable hourly employee cost for copying association records and the price for the copying itself can be assessed by the member requesting the documents.

❖ Disclosure to Non-Members

Under certain circumstances (for example, when a member selling a separate interest requests financial and other information for a prospective buyer who is not a member), the following items are typically provided to the buyer by the current member or association. These may include:

- Copy of the association governing documents
- Any deed or use restriction
- Most recent annual budget report
- Written statement of the association's current regular and special assessments and fees
- Any unpaid assessments levied on the owner's interest in the joint interest development, including any monetary fines or penalties (a demand statement)
- Information on late charges, interest, and costs of collections, if requested
- Copy or summary of any notice previously sent to the owner setting forth any alleged violation of the governing documents that remains unresolved
- Copy of any litigation records that are pending or that have been resolved.
- Any change in the association's current regular and special assessments and fees, which have been approved by the association's board of directors but have not become due and payable as of the date disclosure is provided
- Description of any provision in the governing documents that prohibits the rental or leasing of any of the separate interests in the HOA to a renter lessee or tenant
- Copy of the approved minutes of the meetings of the association's board of directors conducted over the

previous twelve months (excluding executive sessions), if requested by the purchaser.

❖ Timing and Fees for Non-Member Documentation

The association must respond within five (5) days if the owner sends a written request to the association for a payoff request from the association, which is required for a sale or title transfer. An association may collect a reasonable fee for the association's actual cost for the procurement, preparation, reproduction, and delivery of the documents requested.

The fee charged by the management company under its contract constitutes the "actual" cost to the association. The association may not charge additional fees for the electronic delivery of the documents requested. The association or the HOA manager (as an agent of the association) can set the actual cost of changing title records on the transfer of title. This means there are potentially two fees that may be due upon the sale of a property within the standard interest subdivision:

- A reasonable fee for the service of preparing and reproducing all the requested information and documents required by law
- The association's actual cost to change its records related to the transfer of title

❖ Additional Non-Member Requests

Third parties such as lenders, realtors, and underwriters may request information that exceeds state requirements. The board should establish policies and procedures for responding to these requests and the fees to be charged. The most common non-member requests for information are as follows:
- Percentage of owner occupancy
- Description of the common area
- Date of transfer from the declarant
- Present situation regarding litigation
- Condition of the reserve fund

Custodian of Records:

The term "Custodian of Records" in the context of homeowners' associations (HOAs) refers to an individual or entity responsible for maintaining and managing essential records and documents of the HOA The Custodian of Records ensures transparency, compliance, and efficient management of the association's affairs.

The specific responsibilities of a Custodian of Records can vary depending on the HOA's desires. However, some everyday duties typically include:

1. **Document Storage**: The Custodian of Records is responsible for securely storing and organizing important HOA documents, such as financial records, meeting minutes, contracts, bylaws, and rules and regulations. These documents serve as a historical record and are essential for legal and operational purposes.

2. **Record Maintenance**: The Custodian of Records ensures that all records are up-to-date and accurate. This may involve maintaining an organized filing system, tracking changes or updates to documents, and ensuring proper archiving of outdated descriptions.

3. **Record Accessibility**: One of the crucial tasks of the Custodian of Records is to make records accessible to members of the HOA, as required by law or the association's governing documents. This often includes providing access to meeting minutes, financial reports, and other relevant documents upon request.

4. **Compliance and Retention**: The Custodian of Records ensures compliance with applicable laws and regulations concerning recordkeeping and retention. They may be responsible for understanding the legal requirements and timelines for retaining various records and overseeing their proper disposal when necessary.

5. **Record Disclosure**: In some cases, the Custodian of Records may be responsible for responding to requests for information or records from HOA members, potential homebuyers, or third parties. They must follow legal procedures and guidelines for disclosing information while respecting privacy and confidentiality rules.

6. **Support for Board Meetings**: The Custodian of Records

often assists the HOA board by providing necessary documents and records for board meetings. This includes preparing meeting agendas, distributing relevant materials, and archiving meeting minutes.

It's worth noting that the specific title and duties of the Custodian of Records may vary between HOAs. In some cases, the role may be performed by a professional management company hired by the HOA; in others, it may be assigned to a board member or a dedicated staff member within the association.

Maxfield Community Management prefers to operate as the Custodian of Records for every HOA or COA. we manage. This eliminates the boxes and missing information often associated with the board member change and removes the possibility of holding others hostage because of disagreements.

A dedicated Custodian of Records ensures that an HOA maintains proper records, complies with legal requirements, and operates transparently. It helps foster accountability and provides a reliable source of information for HOA members and other persons.

❖ Member and Non-Member Property Provisions

An essential part of community management involves responding correctly and in a timely fashion to member and non-member activities on the property. Unlike owning a single-family detached house outside of an association, where the owner is only limited by the city code and ordnance as to their behavior, restrictions imposed by the HOA limits both member and non-members.

- **Satellite dishes:** As more people ditch cable and choose satellite services, an HOA may limit some aspects of satellite installation as long as it does not significantly increase or decrease the cost, efficiency, or performance of the unit. The board must expedite the request for the satellite and is prohibited from charging a fee or deposit. The HOA has to allow satellite dishes but can make rules about how the installation and where it is to be placed - granted as long it permits the reception of such a signal. The good news is that with high-speed internet - dishes are becoming less common, and streaming platforms are.

- **Signage**: HOAs must comply with the state code and allow members to display a "For sale" sign on their separate interest as long as the character is reasonably located in plain view of the public, is of a reasonable dimension and design as determined by the local jurisdiction and does not adversely affect public safety including traffic safety. The sign may advertise that the separate is for sale, lease, or exchange by the owner or their agent, provide directions to the particular interest, or provide the owner or agent's name, address, and phone number. Political signs are also protected, but the size of the character and the materials may be restricted, and they cannot adversely affect public health and safety or violate local, state, or federal law.

- **Political Signs:** In 2022, Utah bill SB152 prohibited an HOA or COA. from restricting by rule an owner's right to display a political sign in the window of the residence or to regulate the content of the political sign. Additionally, SB152 prevents an HOA in a P.U.D. to prohibit the placement of a political sign on a lot, the exterior of a residence, or the front yard, regardless of whether the HOA has ownership over such area. However, SB152 did allow an HOA or COA. to, by rule, reasonably regulate the time, place, and manner of posting the political sign. According to our law firm, "The most common question resulting from last year's SB152 is "what is a political sign" since many signs could be political in nature? SB191 addresses that question. It defines a political sign as "any sign or document that advocates the election or defeat of a candidate for public office, or the approval or defeat of a ballot proposition." Accordingly, all other types of signs would not be protected as a "political sign" under the statute."

- **Flag displays:** HOAs cannot prevent anyone from displaying the flag of the United States unless it is used as an advertising display.

- **Vehicle towing:** HOAs may have vehicles in the common area towed if they adhere to the requirements found in the towing code. The association must post signage at each entrance outlining what is and what is not allowed, the towing company contact info, and other disclosures. The law even goes as far as describing the icon of the tow truck requirement on the sign.

❖ **Legally Towing Vehicles**

The HOA agent must provide written authorization to the towing company before the towing commences. The written authorization must include the following details:
- Make, model, vehicle identification number, and license plate of the removed vehicle
- Name, signature, job title, residential or business address, and working telephone number of the person described above authorizing the removal of the vehicle
- Grounds for the removal of the vehicle
- Time when the vehicle was first observed parked at the private property
- Time that authorization to tow the vehicle was given

❖ **Monthly Dues**

When you belong to an HOA, you pay monthly dues because a common area must be maintained, and money must be saved for improvements or replacements in the future. In effect, a portion of each monthly due payment goes for current expenses, and the balance goes into a reserve account for future costs. Suppose you own a property without a homeowners' association. In that case, the individual owner must pay for a new roof out of their pocket, but for an association, adequate funds must be available for this expected future expense.

Three types of assessments: Monthly dues are categorized as regular, unique, and individual. Each assessment type has regulations related to approvals, amounts, and notification of members. Unique and special assessments are usually defined in the CC&Rs of your association. These are intended to reimburse the association for funds expended on behalf of any one owner. Here are the differences between regular and special assessments:

- **Regular**: This is the payment made by all members to cover the association's expenses. The Board may approve an annual increase of 20 percent of the regular (typically monthly) assessment without owner approval. If the growth is more than 20 percent of the previous fiscal year, the change requires the support of the majority of quorum (more than 50 percent of owners). The increase must be sent by individual notice thirty to sixty days before the expansion comes due and included in the annual budget report.

- **Special**: This is an additional assessment for a particular purpose determined during the budget process, an additional assessment after the budget has been published, or a new assessment due to an unforeseen expense because of an emergency. If the increase is 5 percent or less of the budgeted annual gross cost, this does not require owner approval, and the Board may approve this increase. If the growth is more than 5 percent (e.g., fifty owners are paying $300 per month or $180,000 in total, the special assessment would be $9,000, or $180 per owner), this increase requires the approval of the majority of the quorum (more than 50 percent of owners). This would be disclosed in the annual notification of possible special assessments by individual notice and sent thirty to sixty days before the particular review is due.

- **Emergency special assessments**: Special assessments for emergencies are not limited. An emergency is defined as any one of the following situations:

- A court-ordered extraordinary expense (e.g., a judgment amount not covered by insurance)
- A necessary repair because of a threat to personal safety on the property (e.g., pool fencing needing immediate replacement)
- An extraordinary expense that could not have been reasonably foreseen by the Board when preparing the budget (e.g., unstable building, fire sprinkler recall, or mold remediation). An extraordinary expense requires a resolution of the Board explaining the reason for the expense and why the expense was not foreseen during the budget process.

Increasing dues (without alienating owners): It is a fact of life that as a board member, at some point you will have to raise the monthly assessment. The reality is that you are not only raising dues on other owners; but ironically, you are also increasing the dues on yourself. Nothing grabs owners' attention in your community more than raising the monthly assessment. It creates tension at meetings, leading to Board recalls and hostile community meetings.

But suppose you do not increase your dues to pay for escalating operating costs, to fund your reserve account better, or to address an imminent repair or system replacement. In that case, you may risk violating your fiduciary duty or forcing a board member to increase. Although shortly a touchy subject and sure to irritate some owners no matter how you justify the increase, here are a few ways to handle communicating an increase in dues:

- **Explain the current situation:** Many owners are just oblivious to the financial position of the community. They do not read the annual budget, attend meetings, or pay attention to the dynamics of your community. It would help if you educated them. Whether at the annual meeting, in a newsletter, or an email to every owner, provide detailed information on the current financial status of your community. Review the reserve study, current bank balances, and operating expenses.

- **Explain the future need:** Many owners do not understand the community's future needs. A portion of the dues paid today pay for repairs required in the future. This is done so there is money to pay for those repairs without imposing a special assessment. If the roof of a community needs to be replaced and there are not sufficient reserves on hand, each owner will have to pay for the cost of their roof and their portion of the common area to be reroofed, and that assessment may run into thousands of dollars. By increasing dues today, you are funding that future expense.

- **Show that you are a good steward:** Do not just accept the reserve study estimates as gospel divined by a third party; obtain quotes for your significant systems and replacement projects from trusted vendors. If the reserve study estimated that the useful life of your roofs is three years and the cost to replace them is $500,000, have a roofing contractor provide their assessment. They may estimate a roof life of seven years and a price to replace of $400,000. They may also recommend a maintenance program that may extend the life of the roofs and save the association some money. Either way, the Board can show they are a good steward of the association's capital, providing reasonable due diligence, and any increase is entirely justified.

- **At least keep up with inflation:** One tactic some associations use is adjusting the dues annually with the inflation rate. If your rights are $300 and the annual inflation rate is 3 percent, you would increase your dues by $9 monthly. This keeps your dues in line with the cost to provide services, and owners will become acclimated and expect an annual increase in their rights. Just as their property tax bill increases yearly by 2 percent, they understand the cost to do business increases annually, which is justifiable and fair.

❖ Removing Reservations about Reserves

Many Home Developers and Builders set up HOAs with artificially low budgets that don't account for the final expenses or undercapitalize the reserve account. After the declarant (developer) turns the HOA over to the members, it is common practice for boards to keep the monthly dues artificially low and then charge a special assessment to cover the costs of big projects. Since the developments are new, there aren't a lot of capital improvements needed, but after about 5-8 years, boards quickly realize the problem with this practice is twofold:

- The low monthly dues were deceptive to new owners. An owner could live in the property with artificially low dues and sell their property. Then, the new buyer would have to pay the entire cost of the improvement or replacement in a special assessment or increased dues.
- Some owners could not afford to pay the short-term special assessment. It was not unusual to have a $500 monthly special assessment paid over twelve months to fund a roof replacement. However, sure owners on a fixed income could not pay the assessment, which triggered late fees, collections, and, in some cases, foreclosure.

To help Boards avoid these issues, Utah law requires HOAs and COAs to have a reserve study done every six years and reviewed every three years. A reserve study identifies the components the association must repair, restore, replace, and maintain, providing an expected cost and timeframe for each. A reserve study must include:
- a list of the components the association is required to repair, replace, restore, or maintain that have a remaining useful life of less than thirty years
- an estimate of the remaining useful life of each component as of the date of the study
- The estimated costs to repair, replace, restore, or

maintain each of the components during and at the end of their useful life
- an estimate of the necessary annual contribution to the reserve to meet the estimated cost of replacing a component.

Here is a list of what may be included in a reserve study:
- Streets
- Roofs
- Painting
- Pools
- Tennis courts

Reserve accounts can run into millions depending on the size of the community and the amenities offered, what the CC&Rs dictate, and what the association covers, not the owner. It is common for districts not to be fully funded, and often, they may be at 25 to 50 percent of the fully funded reserve. Why is that? The reserve study may show the valuable life for a component much shorter than what the Board believes the useful life will be. A reserve study may say the roofs need to be replaced in twenty years, but a roofer who inspects them thinks they will be fine for twenty-five or even thirty years. **The reserve study may have costs to replace or restore components that are much higher than what the current market expense may be.** The reserve study may determine it will cost $8,000 to reroof every townhome, but the Board has a bid from a reputable roofer for $5,000.

❖ **Reserve Fund Expenditures**

Once a reserve fund account is established, those funds cannot be expended for any purpose other than repairing or replacing the major components for which the reserve fund was established. The Board may authorize the temporary transfer of money from a reserve fund to the association's general operating fund to meet short-term cash flow or other expenses, provided the Board has stated the intent to transfer in a meeting notice.

The Board must also issue a written finding recorded in the Board's minutes, explaining why the transfer is needed and describing when and how the money will be repaid to the reserve fund. The Board must include repayment options to the reserve account, including increasing the monthly dues, a special assessment, or even a loan. Still, the explanation must be in the agenda of the board meeting and the minutes. Since the minutes are provided to prospective buyers, owners will be aware of the agenda item, these red flags signal an underfunded reserve account. The civil code requires the repayment of these funds within one year of the initial transfer date. The Board may delay, however, if it makes a finding supported by documentation that a temporary delay would be in the best interest of the HOA.

Notice of a board meeting must include the intent to consider delay in repayment. As is evident in these laws and reporting requirements, the Board must ensure necessary funds in the reserve account and not use the reserve account to fund ongoing operations of the community but to have them used and earmarked for future projects.

Why is a Healthy Reserve Important (To the Board and the Community)?

As the director on the Board, you have a fiduciary responsibility to stay objective, unselfish, responsible, honest, trustworthy, and efficient. Board members, as stewards of public trust, must always act for the good of the organization rather than for the benefit of themselves.

As the director on the Board, you have...One of the most important ways this manifests itself is how the Board chooses to fund their reserves. You do not operate in a vacuum because of how much money is in addition, and the percentage of the fully funded budget is shared with owners, lenders, buyers, and any interested party.

If a director willingly disregards the reserve study recommendations without concrete reasons and the community remains underfunded, you may expose the Board to some legal issues. Here are a few reasons why a healthy reserve is essential:

- **Lenders care:** When a buyer needs financing on a property, they may hold the title to the property, but until the loan is paid off, the lender has a vested interest in the property. If they have to foreclose on the property because of non-payment, the community's condition will impact the property's value, and they may not recoup the loan still on the books and the cost to foreclose. Lenders will review the budget, reserve study and determine if the property and association are worth the risk.

- **Buyers care:** As part of a buyer's due diligence on the purchase of a property in an HOA, the seller is required to provide disclosures on the subject property, including all documentation related to the HOA, such as the budget, minutes, CC&Rs, rules and regulations, and whatever else requested by the buyer. If they discover the reserves are 10 percent of total funding and insufficient money for imminent repairs, they may be inclined to pass on purchasing the property. Suppose the seller does not disclose to the buyer because the Board did not record in the minutes a plan for shoring up the reserves (such as a significant increase in dues, a special assessment, or a bank loan). In that case, the buyer may have legal recourse against the seller or Board for non-disclosure.

- **Emergencies and the unexpected:** Even if your reserve level seems adequate for expected repairs and replacements, you need sufficient reserves for the unexpected. We managed an association whose entire gas line infrastructure had to be replaced immediately because it was red tagged by the gas company. The Board had to come up with $250,000 for this repair directly, and because there was not enough money on hand in reserves, they had to implement a special assessment to fund an emergency loan. This has also happened when there are construction deficiencies. One community in Midvale had to come up with $1.5 Million for repairs from water damage to stucco and decks that were improperly installed.

- **One way or another, you need the money:** The money in the reserve belongs to every owner and is a savings account to fund necessary repairs. If an owner did not live in an association, they would have to come up with the funds to repair their roof or paint the exterior. The money probably would not be sitting in a dedicated reserve account but still would have to be available from some report. The community needs the reserve funds to pay for repairs that an expert has called out in the reserve study that the Board must address. Whether it is a special assessment, a bank loan, or money readily available in the reserves, the Board will need these funds to pay for these repairs.

- **Tell the world why you are fine:** If your reserve funds are not at the level recommended by the reserve study, the Board may have valid reasons to maintain a lower level of funds. Perhaps the remaining life of the roof is longer than that estimated by the study, or the cost to repair or replace the ceiling is lower than that in the study. A prudent board should obtain valid, detailed quotes from a vendor to justify a more insufficient balance. The key is to communicate to your community, and anyone interested in buying or lending that your reserve balance is adequate.

❖ **Current Operating Expenses**

Most of the dues go to future capital expenses, but most rights go toward maintaining the association and paying for current operating costs. Some operational costs of a typical association are as follows:
- Insurance

- Landscaping
- Common Utilities such as water, sewer, and trash
- Snow Removal
- Association management
- Patrol or Guards for gated communities
- Pool service

Every month, the Board will review actual expenses versus expected costs, and every year, the Board, with the assistance of the management company, will create a pro-forma operating budget to be shared with all the owners. This budget may include increasing dues to pay for rising expenses or to increase the reserves. The books and records of the association reflect the decisions of the Board of Directors. Maintaining the books and records is an ongoing process. The financial reports are prepared from the books and records. They should make clear to the Board the adequacy of reserves, the cost of services rendered, and the current condition of the reserve funds.

❖ Ensuring the Association

Mitigating risks and insurance for the HOA is one of the board's most critical responsibilities. There are several different coverages to consider, some of which are mandatory to have:
- Commercial general liability: Protects individual owners from damages sustained in common areas - typical coverage is $2 Million for 100 or fewer units and $3 Million for 101 or more units.
- Directors and Officers' liability: Protects all directors and officers from individual liability related to decisions legally made, as well as the occurrences that happen during their terms in office. This may be void if the director or officer receives compensation.
- Fidelity: Indemnifies the employee, managing agent, and independent contractors in the event of theft or misappropriation of the HOA's assets. Some, but not all, insurance companies will add the HOA's management company to the policy to cover the HOA's funds under this policy.
- Property: Covers the replacement of a building should

it be damaged or destroyed
- Make sure the policy states that the structure's replacement cost is covered. Do not over insure, as the replacement cost may be less than the property's market value.
- Earthquake: Covers repair or replacement cost resulting from earthquake damage
- This must be obtained if required in the governing documents.
- Deductibles can be 10-25% of the value.
- Flood: Provides coverage on residential structures from water damage caused by a flood. Lenders require HOAs in flood plains to obtain this insurance through the National Flood Insurance Program (NFIP) or other sources.

❖ **Annual Meeting**

Almost all homeowners associations in Utah are organized as non-profit corporations, and as such, Utah law requires such associations to hold at least one membership meeting per year. UCA 16-6a-701. This meeting is commonly referred to as the annual meeting. Associations often have multiple sessions throughout the year. The annual conference, however, is specifically required by statute, and it provides an association's members the opportunity to receive a recap of the association's activities from the preceding year and a snapshot of the association's activities for the upcoming year. The annual meeting also provides an association's members an opportunity to chime in and make recommendations for the association's operation, as well as to vote to elect an association's newest members of its Board of directors.

A home owners association's annual meeting provides an association the opportunity to address two additional requirements of Utah law that apply to homeowners associations. First, an association's Board of directors must adopt an annual budget and provide the association's members a summary of the adopted budget. UCA 57-8a-215. The summary provides the association's members information on the association's recurring expenses (i.e., landscaping, utilities, security, etc.), as well as any significant or unusual expenditures (i.e., resurfacing a pool, reroofing buildings, installing playground equipment, etc.) that the association intends to make during the year. In addition, if the association's governing documents do not expressly authorize the Board to adopt an annual budget, the annual meeting allows the association's members to ratify the budget.

Second, and as part of the budget process, the home owners association's Board of directors must complete a reserve analysis of the costs to repair, maintain, and replace the common area and facilities with a useful life of 3 – 30 years. UCA 57-8-7.5; UCA 57-8a-211. The association board must include a line item in the budget for reserve contributions, and the Board must allow owners to veto the reserve line-item amount proposed. If the owners do not reject such reserve provision by a 51% vote of the entire membership within 45 days of the Board's adoption, the proposed budget shall be considered adopted. *Id*.

As mentioned above, a homeowners association may hold meetings in addition to its annual conference throughout the year. But if there is only one association meeting you intend to sit in on during the year, plan on attending the annual meeting, as it is often the most informative and essential.

Usually, the by-laws mandate the location, date, and time of the annual meeting of the members; the Board may fix a date and time by resolution. Best practices are:
- Hold a meeting at the clubhouse or common area in the development or at a location reasonably close.
- Hold the meeting in the spring or fall - summer and holiday season people are busy.

→ **Notice:** Written notice of the meeting shall be given during specific timeframes before the annual meeting date and via specific methods. These requirements supersede notice provisions shorter than may be contained in the by-laws. Notice requirements are no less than 15 Days but no more than 60 days.

→ **Ballots**
- The ballots should be sent 15 days before the meeting by first-class mail. Some associations do a vote at the meeting, which is also acceptable. There are pros and cons to each method.

→ **Distribution**
- Meeting notices should be delivered personally or by first-class mail; notices may be transmitted electronically if requested by a member.
- Electronic notification is permitted if all applicable sections of the code are followed.
- Secret ballots must be distributed by first-class mail and may not be distributed electronically.

→ **Record date**
- Members on the "record date" or notice are entitled to receive notification of association meetings. If the record date is not outlined in the by-laws, the Board may fix a record date no more significant than sixty and no fewer than fifteen days before the annual meeting.
- If no record date for the notice is fixed, those who are members at the close of the business day preceding the day the notice is given are entitled to such information.

→ **Required notice content**
- The notice should include the date, time, and place for the meeting.
- All proposed business should be stated in the notice.
- It should include the names of candidates the association knows if the meeting is timed with a vote to elect directors.
- Relevant information about matters requiring member consent should be included if presented for action at the annual meeting.

Meeting preparation: Good practice warrants including the following additional information in the annual meeting package sent to the members before the annual meeting, whether or not required by the by-laws.

- Agenda
- Draft minutes of the previous membership meetings
- Director and committee member names
- Financial report or budget
- Information regarding agenda items
- Election and voting materials: ballots, double envelopes, and instructions

Items to have at the annual meeting are as follows:

- A copy of all materials sent to members with the meeting notice
- A copy of the budget (and reserve study)
- Sign-in sheet/membership list/registration list
- Agenda
- Election items, if applicable
  - Ballots/double envelopes
  - Voting tally sheets
  - Report of inspector(s) of election

Agenda and minutes: The agenda is the official order of business for a meeting. The Board (with the assistance of management) usually establishes and prioritizes the agenda items for the annual meeting. However, sometimes, the governing documents show the annual agenda.

→ Agenda content
  - Election of directors
  - Annual board and committee reports
  - Approval of previous year's annual meeting minutes
  - Annual Federal Revenue Ruling 70-604 vote
  - Member comment (or homeowners' open forum) Other matters the Board intends to present for action

→ Minutes: The corporation must retain minutes of all its meetings, including those of its members. It is good practice to submit the minutes of the membership meeting to the Board for approval at its first meeting following the membership meeting. The minutes may also be presented to the membership for approval at the next meeting. Once approved, the secretary should sign the minutes.

Meeting procedures: The civil code requires annual and special meetings of the association's membership to be conducted by a recognized system of parliamentary procedure. These procedures may be predefined (e.g., Robert's Rules or as identified and adopted by the Board). The Board should adopt procedural rules before the membership meeting.

Chair of the annual meetings: Often, the president of the association, or in their absence, the vice president or another officer, will chair the meeting. However, anyone can chair an appointment if needed.

The quorum for member meetings: A "quorum" describes the minimum number of members that must participate either in person, by proxy, or by ballot at a conference for any official action to occur. Quorum is usually defined in the by-laws as a percentage of the total number of votes that may be cast, which can sometimes be different than the total number of members in the association.

Once the minimum number is achieved, the actual number of represented memberships may also be called a "quorum." This distinction is essential where matters presented for action require approval of the "majority of the quorum."

Once a quorum is established, the members can continue to do business even if members leave the meeting and those present no longer represent a quorum.

Reduced quorum: Some by-laws authorize reducing the number of memberships constituting a quorum if the original cannot be met. This reduced quorum (aka step-down quorum) is intended to permit action that would otherwise be prohibited owing to insufficient member representation.

The reduced option is permitted only if authorized in the by-laws.

For those member meetings where a quorum is not present, then generally, another appointment can be scheduled within the next few days, and the persons that show up to that meeting would constitute a quorum unless

Election process:
All elections should provide equal access to association media and meeting space to communicate election issues.
- Specific qualifications for candidates and nomination procedures
- Specific qualifications for voting
- Authenticity, validity, and effect of proxies
- Specific voting periods for elections, including poll operating hours
- Specific methods of selecting inspector(s) of elections

If there is a conflict between election rules and the by-laws, the by-laws control. However, if not, the election rules will control. Here are a few elections best practices:
- Adopt election rules consistent with the governing documents.
- Adopt fair procedures for self-nomination (within election rules).
- Use the secret ballot process for all member votes.
- Seek an amendment to the by-laws to reduce or eliminate the quorum for the annual meeting and reduce the quorum for the election of directors.

Cumulative voting: Typically, at an election, a member is entitled to cast one vote for each vacancy being filled on the Board. For example, if three director seats are for election, each member can cast three votes. If cumulative voting is permitted, each member may cast more than one vote for any candidate up to the total number of votes they are entitled to. Thus, in our example, a member may cumulate two votes for one candidate and cast one vote for another, or the member may cumulate all three votes for a single candidate.

The association should hold a meeting at which a member may announce their intent to cumulate votes. This can be accomplished at the board meeting before the annual meeting. It is standard practice to follow a set of agenda items for that meeting, including the announcement of intent to cumulate votes, appoint inspectors, set a record date, set an annual meeting date, etc. The law states that every member entitled to vote at any election of directors may cumulate their votes only if:

- The governing documents do not prohibit cumulative voting
- The candidates' names were placed in nomination before the voting
- A member has given notice at a meeting of his intention to cumulate votes.

Typically, cumulative voting needs to be explained on the ballot. However, the announcement of a member's intent to cumulate votes may be made at the meeting held to count and tabulate votes, as long as the information is made before the polls are closed ("before voting"). Suppose an association intends to close polls before the date or time of the tabulation meeting. In that case, it may be necessary to hold a separate meeting to allow a member to announce their intent to cumulate votes.

❖ Inspector(s) of Elections

In some states, Inspectors are brought in. While not a requirement in Utah - it's worth mentioning as we will get here someday. One or three election inspectors will be appointed to oversee the elections. Inspectors may not receive compensation and perform the following duties unless allowed under law or by the governing documents:

- Oversee the collection, opening, and tabulation of votes or ballots
- Verify quorum, including any reduced quorum provisions
- Receive, manage, and maintain custody of sealed envelopes and ballots (and proxies, if allowed and used)
- Certify the results of the election or vote by preparing and signing a report of the inspector(s) of elections after the ballots are counted and tabulated

- Determine which directors are elected and for what term length
- Maintain the ballots and election materials for at least one year
- Complete other duties as defined in election rules

Election process: Some boards find the election process complicated and burdensome, so they outsource this task to their management company while overseeing the results. Here is the entire process to be carried out before the election:
- Verify and implement election rules
- Determine the number of open director positions and term lengths
- Send out a "Call for Nominations" package (in time to include nominee names in voting materials)
- Verify candidates' qualifications and standing (hold hearings to suspend voting privileges, if necessary)
- Determine record date for notice and voting purposes
- Appoint one to three inspector(s) of elections (must meet qualifications in the election rules)
- Have inspectors designate ballot return location (including date, operating hours, and poll locations if applicable)
- Distribute meeting notice with voting package

Voting package: The voting package must be distributed at least thirty days before the close of polls and should include the following elements:
- Cover letter and instructions
- Annual meeting notice
- Ballots and double envelopes (to maintain confidentiality and the proper number of votes per member)
- Candidate statements (optional unless governing documents state otherwise)
- Proxies (optional unless governing documents state otherwise)
- Advertisements for a candidate information session, if applicable and desired (optional unless governing documents state otherwise)

The process to be carried out after the election is as follows:
- Announce results to members (at the meeting when tabulated and in writing within fifteen days)
- Add certified results to the association's records (completed and signed inspector's report, ballots, election materials)
- Record election results in the board meeting minutes
- Seat directors
- Hold short organizational board meeting (immediately after the annual meeting or at the next board meeting)
- Assign directors to corporate officer positions for the following year (adequately documented in the agenda)

Who Can Be on the Board?

A board of directors election is conducted when there are vacancies or if the board declares the office of a director vacant because the director:
- has been found of unsound mind by a final order of the court
- has been convicted of a felony
- fails to meet the qualifications provided in the by-laws and election rules.

Generally, the by-laws and election rules require a director to be a "member in good standing." Before someone can be deemed not in good standing, they must be notified of the reasons and a hearing. You always need to notify affected individuals and allow them the opportunity to bring themselves into good standing.

These same rules apply to qualifications applicable to candidates for the board. Associations must adopt election rules that state the capabilities of directors. Stuff in the election rules should be consistent with those outlined in other governing documents. Associations must allow members to self-nominate. Some governing documents prohibit members from serving on the board if they are not on title to the property. I have also seen rules that say you must occupy the property, but I don't think this would hold up if challenged. Additionally, nominations may be completed via any of the following methods:

- Nominating committee
- Board recruiting
- General solicitation
- Writing in candidates on the ballot
- "Request for Candidate" forms sent by the association
- Other reasonable nomination procedures
- From the floor of the member meeting (if election and member meeting are timed appropriately)

Director terms: The by-laws set the terms of the directors and the number of authorized directors. A director holds office until the expiration of his time and until a successor has been elected and qualified. The articles or by-laws may allow staggered terms of directors to provide continuity on the board. A board meets to make decisions and communicate those decisions with their members. These meetings may be called differently due to the intent of the meeting. Directors hold a 2 to 3 year term, three years being ideal.

Special member meetings: Annual meetings address predictable business matters. In contrast, special meetings of the members are scheduled to address unforeseen events as mentioned below:

- Amendments of governing documents (CC&Rs, by-laws, etc.)
- Approval of capital improvements or expenditures
- Election of directors to replace those recalled by the membership or a court
- Removal of directors with a recall
- Votes on grant of exclusive use of common area
- Votes on special assessments or assessment increases

Annual and special meetings: These two types of meetings share similar guidelines:

- The meeting location is designated in the by-laws or the corporation's office.
- Members are notified as specified in the by-laws, but generally, by one of the following means:
  - First-class or other form of mail delivery
  - Personal delivery
  - Newspaper

- o Electronic notification (only with member consent)
- All members as of the record date receive Notice.
- A copy of the proof of Notice is sent by the manager or association office by certified mail or as an affidavit by the secretary.
- The quorum and adjournment are specified in the governing documents.

Annual Notice of Meeting: The date and time of a special session are determined by the association documents or the non-profit corporation act, which requires at least ten days. Suppose you mail the Notice other than first-class or registered mail at least 30 days and more than 60 days before the meeting date. You can also provide notices in a newspaper, but who ads those anyway?

Best Practice: Set your meeting early and notify everyone about 30-45 days before the meeting. This gives people the opportunity to schedule and attend. The goal is to set a meeting date and time that the most significant number will attend.

Special Meeting Notices:
Unlike the annual meeting, special meetings are generally urgent, and unless the bylaws provide for a longer or shorter period, at least two days' notice is typically required.
The Notice must state the following details of the special meeting:
- Time and date
- Location
- General nature of the business to be conducted

No business may be transacted or voted upon at a special meeting beyond that included in the Notice.

Meeting procedures: These procedures are similar to those of an annual meeting:
- Parliamentary procedures
- Minutes
- Chair for special meetings
- Quorum for special meetings
- Inspector(s) of elections for special meetings (required for recalls)

- Ballots for special meetings (required for recalls)
- Voting at special meetings (required for recalls)
- Close of special meetings

The quorum for the special meeting: Once a quorum is obtained by people in attendance or returned ballots, determination of the percentage or number of votes needed to approve or disapprove an action may be necessary (e.g., a simple majority, a majority of "all" members, supermajority).

Here are some of the differences between annual and special meetings:

❖ **Board Meetings**

A board meeting is defined in the corporation code as either a congregation of a majority of the members of the board at the same time to hear, discuss, or deliberate upon any item of business that is within the authority of the board or a teleconference in which a majority of the members of the board, in different locations, are connected by electronic means through audio or video or both. There are three types of board meetings:

→ Open: For all predictable business within the board's authority, either a regular or special meeting. Regular open meetings occur periodically, such as the first Monday of the month, but special meetings occur on a date other than that regularly scheduled meeting.

→ Emergency: For unforeseen issues requiring immediate attention, such as property damage.

→ Executive session: For sensitive issues inappropriate for open session, for example, disciplinary actions. Executive sessions of the board are not held independently, but instead, they follow or precede a regular board meeting. They address:
  - litigation and anything protected by attorney-client privilege
  - formation of contracts with third parties
  - member discipline
  - personnel matters (e.g., hiring or firing)
  - requests by delinquent members for assessment

payment plans
- initiation foreclosure
- action and guidelines.

Action through board meetings: Sometimes, board members take steps outside of board meetings, such as meeting to discuss landscaping and telling the landscaper to add or remove something. While this can be done this way or via text and email, the Board needs to approve and document all actions taken at the next board meeting right after reviewing and approving the minutes.

Remote meetings: Thanks to COVID-19, boards hold many meetings by Zoom (or equivalent). The board may hold a remote meeting in which most members, or all members in different locations, are connected via electronic means with audio and video. Participation in a remote meeting (e.g., teleconference or web conference) constitutes a presence in person at that meeting, provided that:
- Each director can communicate with all others concurrently
- Each director can participate in all matters before the board
- The association adopts and implements some means of verifying
  - The person communicating remotely is a director entitled to participate in the board meeting;
  - All statements, questions, actions, or notes are made by that director and not an unauthorized person.
- Except for a meeting held solely in executive session, Notice of the remote meeting is given to all members so they can attend.

Notice requirements: Meeting notice requirements are individually specified for directors and members.

Notice	Board of Directors	Members
Regular/Annual	No notice if fixed in by-laws or board	Fixed in by-laws, otherwise: 4 days by notice
Special	Unless the articles or by-laws provide, otherwise: 4 days via mail, 48 hours via phone, voicemail, email, or fax	4 days by general notice
Emergency	Whatever is feasible under the circumstances	Not required since impractical owing to immediate necessity
Executive Session	4 days via mail, 48 hours via phone, voicemail, email, or fax	2 days by general notice
Waiver	Directors may provide a written waiver of notice	N/A

Agenda and minutes: The board sets a unique plan for each meeting to establish the business under consideration. During a non-emergency session, the board may bring up and discuss or take action on any item of business not included on the Agenda published with the Notice, with limited exception. If a Board considers rule amendments or things associated with fees, dues, fines, or special assessments, those items must be on the Agenda before the Notice.

An association is required to keep a record of its proceedings, including meetings of the board. Copies of the minutes must be available for inspection by the members in draft form within thirty days of the meeting. Minutes signed by the association's secretary are deemed prima facie evidence of the truth of the matters outlined in the minutes. On the contrary, minutes of an executive meeting are not required to be available to members. They may, however, need to be produced in response to a lawful subpoena. The minutes may be prepared by a board member or management company but must accurately reflect the actions taken by the board.

Adjournment of board meetings: Adjournment procedures to close a meeting of the board for either of the following reasons:
- Business is concluded.
- It must be continued at a new place, date, and time because
  - If a quorum is not achieved
  - business is not concluded to the satisfaction of the board.

Executive session hearings: When the board meets in an executive session to consider and impose discipline upon a member, that member is entitled to Notice, to attend the session, and to address the board. Ten days before the meeting, notice must be given and conform to the fundamental due process requirements. If the by-laws provide more extended Notice, this notice date must be followed. The Notice must state:
- The date, time, and place of the meeting
- that the member may attend and address the board
- the nature of the alleged violation.

It is also good practice to include statements about the potential discipline that may be imposed:
- Imposition of a reimbursement assessment
- Levying of a fine
- Suspension of the right to vote
- Suspension of standard area privileges

If the board imposes discipline, written Notice must be provided by either personal delivery or first-class mail within fifteen days following the action.

Association member rights: The Open Meeting Act outlines members' specific rights regarding board meetings.
Attendance: Members may attend board meetings not held in executive session, including teleconference meetings. Remote meetings must be audible to members at a location specified in the Notice.
Executive session business: This needs to be shown on the Agenda and "generally noted" in the minutes of the meeting immediately following the next open session meeting of the board.
Board meeting minutes: Members must be told of their right to copies and the methods for obtaining them, which must be included in the annual policy statement distributed to all members.
Meeting notice: Notice must be given to the members by general delivery under the civil code or by individual delivery if requested by the member. Information must include an agenda and may also be delivered via newsletter, public mailing, or the website.
Emergency meetings: The association president or two directors may call an emergency meeting.
Speaking rights: Members have the right to speak at any meeting of the membership and the board except at an executive session of the board. The board may set reasonable time limits for each member to speak.

❖ **Committee Meetings**

More larger associations use committees to advise the board on policies, information, and actions to be taken. Although the board may delegate some authority to a committee, the responsibility for any action taken remains with the board unless the governing documents authorize the committee to act. There are three types of committees:
- Required (or Executive): This is composed of the board of directors.
- Standing: These committees have ongoing tasks and last indefinitely (e.g., architectural).
- Ad hoc: These committees have limited duration and

are formed to address a specific issue (i.e., a rules committee that recommends how the association's operating rules should be modified to address a specific issue).

Each committee should have a charter that describes its purpose, the authority extended to it, budgetary limits on its operation, composition, quorum requirements, and requirements for reporting to the board (e.g., the time, place, and manner of calling committee meetings). Committees of the board, which include two or more directors and are set up per the corporation code's requirements (aka, an executive committee), must keep minutes. Additionally, the Davis-Stirling Act requires committees with "decision-making authority" to keep minutes. Associations should consult legal counsel to confirm which of their committees, if any, must keep minutes.

Benefits of committees: Although each committee serves a specific function, the overarching purpose of all HOA committees is to lighten the workload of the board members. The board has many roles and responsibilities and requiring them to handle every community aspect can quickly overwhelm them. They may need to pay more attention to specific duties. The board can share the burden and delegate particular tasks by forming committees.

A dedicated committee can also help speed up the completion of work. Apart from this, committees encourage participation from the members of the association. Many communities struggle to promote engagement, but committees present the perfect opportunity to get members involved. They allow members to contribute to the association, making them feel helpful and needed and increasing homeowner satisfaction in the community. For associations that struggle to attract participation in board leadership, committees also act as a way to identify future directors for the board. Here are a few joint committees:

Architectural committee: CC&Rs will typically define the purpose of an architectural committee. An architectural committee, or an architectural review or control committee, enforces the community's architectural standards. This committee reviews proposals for modifications, approving or denying them according to the architectural committee guidelines outlined in the CC&Rs. An architectural committee is one of the most important committees in the HOA because, without one, the community risks losing its uniform aesthetics and may suffer from diminishing curb appeal, which may lower property values.

→ **Architectural committee or architectural review process and procedures:** Most governing documents require an owner to seek permission from the association before altering the joint area or separate interest property. In such situations, the Davis-Stirling Act imposes specific "due process" requirements:
  - An association must provide a "fair, reasonable, and expeditious" procedure for making its decision. This procedure must, at a minimum:
    o Include prompt deadlines
    o State the maximum time for a response to an application for approval or reconsideration by the board.

  - The decision on the proposed architectural change must
    o be made "in good faith"
    o not be unreasonable, arbitrary, or capricious
    o Be consistent with any governing law, including the Fair Employment and Housing Act, building code, or other applicable law governing land use or public safety.

  - The decision must be in writing, and if the proposed change is disapproved, it must include:
    o An explanation as to why it was disapproved
    o A description of the procedure for reconsidering the decision by the board of directors.

If a proposed change is disapproved, "the applicant is entitled to reconsideration by the board of directors that made the decision" at an open board meeting. However, the applicant is not entitled to reconsideration if the original decision was made by the board or a group that has the same membership as the board at a meeting held by the civil code. To maximize proper procedure, the Notice approving or denying an application should be based on the reasons and criteria provided for in the governing documents. Special procedures under Civil Code 4765 are as follows:

- Architectural committees are required to keep meeting minutes.
- Architectural decisions must be in writing.
- If the proposed change is disapproved, the Notice of the decision sent to the homeowner must:
    - Include an explanation of why the proposed change was not approved
    - Describe the procedure for reconsidering the decision by the board.
- If an application is denied, associations must have a procedure to allow homeowners to appeal the architectural committee's decision to the board.
- Associations are required annually to mail a notice to all homeowners describing the association's application process.
- The governing documentation may impose other requirements, such as a Notice to neighbors.

Landscaping Committee: Landscaping is essential to any homeowners' association, as it helps beautify the neighborhood and retain property values. Smaller communities may do without a landscaping committee since many standard amenities exist. More prominent associations, however, may benefit significantly from this type of committee. They are responsible for researching landscaping companies, securing bids, and interviewing candidates. They coordinate with the chosen company, oversee the landscaping work, and provide the board with progress updates. They may determine which types of plants to install, which trees to remove or trim, and the timing for mulching or landscaping replacement.

Budget Committee: Members of this committee assist the board with planning the annual budget. There can also be sub-committees responsible for reserve studies and investments. Since the work of this board generally involves finances, members should have some level of familiarity with the subject matter.

Social/Events Committee: Building a sense of community in a homeowners' association is essential. One way to accomplish that is to organize events and social gatherings that promote community camaraderie. Such events are best left in the hands of a social committee. Members of this committee can conduct polls to find out which events residents are interested in and can handle the execution of the event. This committee should be responsible for making event announcements both online and offline.

Welcome Committee: Moving into a new community can be intimidating and daunting. This committee makes new residents feel more at home, making the transition process more manageable. They may drop by and greet new homeowners, show them the community's amenities, and familiarize the new homeowners with the community's rules and processes.

Newsletter Committee: If your association sends out regular newsletters to residents, it will help to organize a newsletter committee for the job. They format the newsletter, write content, and work with the management company to distribute copies to all homeowners. The board should review the newsletter before distribution to avoid the risk of any potential liability.

Social Media Committee: Many communities are moving to digital format when communicating with homeowners. The power of social media is evident, and a society would be wise to leverage it. This committee helps moderate online forums and social media pages, ensuring all members follow specific ground rules. Additionally, this committee can be responsible for posting announcements and updates to keep all members informed.

Safety Committee: Safety is paramount in any community. By forming a safety committee, the community can work with local law enforcement and private safety companies to maintain that safety. This committee can oversee the creation and operation of a neighborhood watch program.

❖ Homeowner Forums

Homeowner forums are generally held before or after the business portion of the board meeting. They are the period set aside for owner comments, concerns, etc. Though not part of the Agenda, they can be on the meeting notice with the period specified for the forum. Homeowner forums often set the tone for the business meeting. For example, the business meeting may be the same if the discussion has been particularly contentious. Boards can publish guidelines on how the media will be conducted and how owners must conduct themselves. The policies can include how many speakers will be recognized (e.g., submit a speaker's request slip) or the time allotted for each speaker (e.g., three minutes per speaker). Behavior by owners and the board should be respectful and businesslike. The board must allow members of the association the opportunity to speak at board and membership meetings. However, the law does not require member comments to occur at any particular time or for any specific length; this means the board can prohibit member comments during the business portion of the meeting.

❖ Budget and Collections

Annual budget report (aka pro forma budget): Unless otherwise stated in the governing documents, the association shall make available, by individual delivery, an annual budget report thirty to ninety days before the end of its fiscal year. It must include the following information:

- A pro forma operating budget
- A summary of the association's reserves
- A summary of the reserve funding plan adopted by the board
- A statement as to whether the board has determined to defer or not undertake repairs or replacement or any major component with a remaining life of thirty years or less
- A statement as to whether the board, consistent with the reserve funding plan, anticipates that the levy

of one or more special assessments will be required along with the estimated amount, commencement date, and duration of the assessment

- A statement as to the mechanism by which the board will fund reserves to repair or replace major components
- A general statement addressing the procedures used for the calculation and establishment of those reserves to defray the future repair, replacement, or additions to major components
- A statement as to whether the association has any outstanding loans with an original term of more than one year
- A summary of the association's insurance policies
- The Assessment and Reserve Funding Disclosure Summary accompanying each annual budget report or summary of the annual budget report.

How Do You Adopt a Budget (Without Breaking the Bank)?

Adopting the annual budget is the most essential duty of a director. Owners in your community may need to be made aware of much of what you do. Still, they will notice when their monthly dues are increased, typically when the new budget is adopted at the end of the fiscal year unless the board has approved a special assessment for some unforeseen expense during the year. The panel will be exposed to a lot of information for this exercise, and it is critical that the board spend time and energy digesting this information and crafting a budget for the following year. Here is the information that should be reviewed:

Expected expenses: In last year's budget, you estimated costs for this year. How accurate were you? Why were you off? Typically, you can count on a high level of certainty for contractual expenses such as insurance, landscaping, and pool maintenance. Other costs, such as utilities, are more variable and complex. If there has been a consistent anomaly in the expenses, you may need to reconsider the amount of your operating costs.

Actual expenses: You will compare your costs budgeted with your actual expenses. What caused the variance? Certain items, such as emergency repairs, cannot be anticipated. But if you are paying for the same "unexpected" expenses every year, you may want to consider them an expected cost. One association we manage has a problem with people outside the community dumping trash in their community, and they must pay to remove it. It is not a one-time occurrence but happens like clockwork every month, so they should consider this an ongoing expense and budget for it.

Future expenses: Are you aware of projects the community must undertake in the coming year that must paid for in the budget? Should the board charge a special assessment or increase dues substantially if insufficient reserve funds are on hand? If you know you have a substantial expense in the coming year, you must budget for it, have funds to pay the vendor, and preferably have funds out of a fully funded reserve account for this project.

Reserve study: This is a critical part of the budget process. Because your monthly dues pay for the current operating expenses, are you putting enough money away monthly into your reserve account? If the reserve study estimates that your roofs must be replaced for $200,000, will you have those funds on hand in two years? If not, you may need to increase the dues for the next two years to pay for that; otherwise, you may vote for an extensive special assessment in two years. You could have a vendor provide a bid now that is lower than the $200,000, or they can do maintenance work that extends the roof's life until you have sufficient funds in a roof reserve account.

Savings: It is usually at budgeting time that the board analyzes expenses, particularly your big-ticket items such as landscaping, insurance, and perhaps your management fee. Can you get comparable services for less money? Your community does not need to be painted every twenty years; this expense can wait. Put some of these services out to bid and see if you can save some money for your community. In some extreme cases, boards have changed their CC&Rs so that the owners now pay expenses borne by the community. An HOA we managed changed their CC&Rs, so the garage door maintenance and replacement became the owner's responsibility, not the association's, thus saving them a lot of money.

Inflation: Even if you nailed your budget, spent the appropriate amount for operating expenses, and funded your reserves to a healthy level, you still need to consider inflation. If the consumer price index reflects an inflation rate of 3 percent and your monthly dues are $300, you must increase rights by $9 to keep pace with inflation. Not only will your operating costs keep pace with inflation, but the costs for which your reserve accounts are dedicated will also increase. We have not found a community with too much money in its reserve account. Still, we know many associations that need to be funded and prepared for the unexpected.

Collections: Monthly assessments billed and become delinquent are unsecured and do not have a lien initially recorded against the property. But suppose the owner continues not to pay their dues. The debt may become secured when a lien is recorded and perfected against the monies owed. Here are the stages in assessment debt collection:
1. Delinquency: statement or courtesy letter sent to the owner
2. Notice: A pre-lien letter was sent to the owner
3. Lien: a lien recorded against the property
4. Foreclosure: Foreclosure filed
5. Write-off: lousy debt is written off or collected

1. Delinquency: Assessments are delinquent fifteen days after they come due unless the declaration provides a more extended period. Once an assessment is outstanding, the association may elect to recover:
- reasonable costs incurred in the collection, including reasonable attorney's fees
- a late charge
- interest on delinquent balances

2. Pre-lien letter: At least thirty days before the recording of a lien to collect the debt that is past due, the association is required to notify the owner(s) of record in writing, by certified mail, of the following information:
- ➢ Fee and penalty procedures of the association (a copy of the delinquency policy)

- ➢ Itemized statement of charges owed
- ➢ Statement that the owner is not liable to pay the charges, interest, and costs of collection if it is determined the assessment was paid on time
- ➢ Right to request a meeting with the board
- ➢ Name(s) of owner(s) of record
- ➢ Right to participate in informal dispute resolution or alternative dispute resolution

3. Lien: Many delinquencies result in a recorded lien against the debtor's property.

> **Securing debt:** A board should always record an assessment lien when a member becomes delinquent to secure the debt. If a lien is not registered, the debt remains unsecured.
>
> **Timing of the lien:** Timing is outlined in the delinquency control policy of the association. The release of the lien must be recorded within twenty-one days after an owner has paid all sums specified in the lien.
>
> **Authorizing the lien:** The authorization to lien an owner occurs via a resolution during the regular session. The lien must be noted in the minutes without identifying the homeowner by name (i.e., account number or parcel number).
>
> **What to include:**
> - A general description of collection and lien enforcement procedures that detail the amount of the assessment and other sums imposed, a legal report, or the owner's interest against which the evaluation and other aggregates are levied.
> - The record owner's name of the separate interest against which the lien is imposed.
> - The name and address of the trustee authorized by the association to enforce the lien by sale.

4. Foreclosure: The last stage in the collection process is the foreclosure of the separate interest. There are several critical elements to consider related to foreclosure:

Is the foreclosure financially beneficial to the association? Is there enough equity in the property to justify the expense of the foreclosure?

Understand the options available to the association when a senior lien holder forecloses. The association may be in second or third position to lenders and delinquent property taxes, so their lien must be paid off in a foreclosure if there is equity.

Consider the type of foreclosure: judicial or non-judicial. In Utah, most foreclosures are completed non-judicially.

5. Write-off: Sometimes, an association will experience cases of uncollectible assessments. For example, an owner could file bankruptcy or suffer a foreclosure; there is not enough equity to pay off the lien. The criteria for writing off uncollected assessments should be part of the association's delinquency policy adopted by the board. Several factors are involved in the decision to write-offer lousy debt:

- All reasonable methods of collection have been exhausted.
- A determination has been made that the cost to continue collection efforts is not worth the probability of collecting.
- The board votes to approve the write off

❖ Vendors

The quality of your vendors will directly reflect on your community's condition. Finding dependable, cost-effective, and legally compliant vendors to protect your community from lawsuits and negligence is critical. Vendors value the business of HOAs because it is consistent work, associations have the means to pay on time, and, depending on the size of the community and the service provided, the community may be one of the vendor's more prominent clients.

Some more prominent associations have employees who only work for the community. The management company or community must follow all state employment regulations and provide workers' compensation insurance. It is not uncommon for govt agencies to routinely audit companies and management companies for compliance with this law and withholding of taxes.

In Utah, for all earnings over $600, the vendor receives a 1099 from the management company for all payments in that tax year, and a copy of that 1099 is filed with the IRS. Even though these vendors are independent contractors, the association may still be liable for claims against the HOA. For any vendor, the board should have on file the following documentation:

- Business license: Certain vendors must be licensed to be paid for their work. The board should have a copy of the business license on file if required; otherwise, the work performed may not be covered by insurance if not completed correctly.
- Workers' compensation: All Utah employers must carry workers' compensation insurance for their employees, including independent contractors who have employees. An association may consider taking a workers' compensation policy, even if the HOA only uses independent contractors to insulate themselves from employee litigation.
-

Picking one vendor over another: Vendors want association business, but selecting one vendor from many can be daunting. A board's due diligence applies to all contractors, from the professional management company to the association's attorney to the person who cleans the pool weekly. If the association is under professional management, the management company should have several vendors whom they trust and can be recommended. Hiring a poor vendor may mean additional expenses to do the job right, unnecessary costs, poor quality, and a longer completion time. Every vendor reflects the board's decision, and it seems to your owners that the board is not spending association funds effectively or efficiently.

There is no guarantee that a contractor hired by the board will provide the expected job performance. Still, by having a hiring process and doing all the due diligence necessary to select the best contractor, the board insulates from criticism from the community. The membership must then accept that reasonable due diligence was performed, the committee made every attempt to select the best vendor, and any deficiencies lie with the contractor.

Like any decision, there is a balance between the price bid and the expected quality of the work to be completed. There is a saying that the most expensive word in the dictionary is "cheap," and selecting a vendor only on the lowest price quoted may be fraught with considerable risk. For smaller projects, a formal bid process may not be necessary, and the board can rely on the recommendation of the management company or references from the vendor to decide. If the vendor does not perform as promised, the cost to the association for this work is minimal. However, if the project size is large and is significant to the community, the board should institute a formal contract process.

Contract process: To ensure the board is comparing apples to apples for a large project, the board should adopt a process to consider all contracts. One such process is the request for proposal (RFP). Some essential terms and conditions should be included in every contract, such as indemnity and insurance with an additional insured endorsement naming the HOA and the management company. The following details should be included in the RFP:

- Price
- Schedule and availability to start work within the HOA's time requirements
- Evidence of insurance
- Additional insured endorsement
- Check references and material suppliers
- Exceptions to the terms and conditions outlined in the draft contract

Pre-qualification for bidder: If a board insists on soliciting bids from a bidder with no prior experience in the HOA industry, it will require the management company to take the time to thoroughly pre-qualify that bidder:

→ Visit the Contractors State License Board (DOPL) website. http://dopl.utah.gov
- Verify the proper license and requisite insurance.
- Identify any record of complaints.
- Review contractor and company background.
  - Identify when the contractor received their license.

- o Identify if the company owners hold other licenses or own other companies.
- o Identify any previous name/identity changes and discuss reasons with the contractor.
- o Call all bidder references to determine whether work was completed on time and within budget.
- o Solicit a list of material suppliers to confirm the bidder has a positive history of timely payments.

Essential contract provisions: The risk management tools that should be required in any RFP are as follows:

- Clauses describing indemnity relationships between the contracting parties should be included. Indemnification provides that, in the event of a lawsuit, the contractor will "indemnify, defend and hold harmless the HOA, the HOA management company, including all legal fees, expert fees and costs." If the clause does not include the HOA management company, a third party can (and likely will) file suit against the manager and HOA management company, who will then tender it back to the HOA under the terms of the management contract (where the association indemnifies the management company).
- The nature and limits of general liability insurance should be stated. The HOA should be named as additionally insured. No work should commence until the insurance information is submitted correctly.
- The HOA should be named as additionally insured, but it is not unusual for the contractor's insurance company to seek additional payments. The contractor must either include this cost in their bid, or the board can approve to reimburse if warranted.

There are two types of insurance for which additional insured endorsements should be obtained:

- General liability: This covers damage that occurs during work performance.
- Completed operations coverage: This covers damages

that arise after the work is complete. For example, two years after a roof is installed, a leak and a unit are damaged.

Retention funds: This is money retained by the HOA for a specified percentage of each payment made by the HOA during the work. The retention percentage, typically 10 percent of the project price, is released only once the primary contractor proves that all lien claimants (subcontractors, vendors, or material suppliers) have been paid. Under Utah law, retention funds must be released within forty-five days of the contractor's substantial project completion.

Bonding rate: Determine if the contractor can obtain a performance and material bond for the project (two separate bonds typically issued together as one bond, as a percentage of the contract price) and identify the contractor's bonding rate. A bonding rate greater than 2 percent should be reviewed with the contractor. The higher the percentage cost of the bond, the more risk the bonding company has assigned to the contractor.

Award recommendation: After receiving all bids, they must be reviewed to determine the successful bidder. The process of analyzing proposals is referred to as "conditioning." While a low price is perhaps the most compelling component, it is not the only one. Here are some factors to consider:
- Price
- Bond Rate
- Schedule
- Manpower and Supervision
- Insurance
- Qualifications including experience and references

Contract award: Once the board has decided on a contractor, there is still a process to follow:
- Identify the successful bidder.
- Complete the draft contract with essential information from the bidder's quote.
- Ask a legal counsel to review the contract.
- Prepare two originals for signing.

- The board (or board's designee) and the contractor each sign and retain an original signed copy of the contract for their records.

Contract completion: Once the final check is written to the contractor, that contractor is on to the next job, so a board must accept the work as final before releasing the retention funds. Once the contractor submits a written notice of job completion to the board, the board may reject the Notice and issue a punch list of unacceptable or incomplete work. Call a meeting of all parties involved to produce invoices and payment records for review. If issues cannot be resolved quickly, contact a legal counsel to ensure the HOA's rights are protected. If the board accepts the Notice, and the contractor issues a final notice of completion, final payment is made, and retention funds are released.

SECTION 6

ASSOCIATION MANAGEMENT

"If you think it's expensive to hire a professional, wait until you hire an amateur."

Red Adair

❖ Community Manager Responsibilities

Managing an association takes time and expertise, and since a board member can only be paid or receive a financial benefit without losing their insurance protection, most associations with more than ten owners hire a professional association management company. According to the civil code, a "managing agent" is a person or entity that, for compensation, exercises control over the assets of a HOA.

This does not include a full-time employee of the association, a full-time employee of any regulated financial institution operating within its everyday regulated business practice, or anyone who acts on behalf of its principal, the association. While many states require a license, an association manager must not be licensed to practice and manage a community in Utah.

If your association manager does not hold any licenses, I recommend proceeding cautiously. That doesn't mean having a license makes you more competent; it just means you may have higher accountability. Many significant industry associations teach best practices, such as The Community Associations Institute (CAI), which is a nationwide organization of forty thousand members, offers an Association Management Specialist (AMS) credential and a Professional Community Association Manager (PCAM) designation. The National Association of Property Managers (NARPM) also has some of the country's best and most talented managers.

❖ Community Manager's Role and Responsibilities

The managing agent relationship is contractual between the board of directors and the agent or management firm. Financially related duties of the managing agent (or bookkeeper, if outsourced) include
- Collecting and disposing of association funds
- Assisting the board in understanding their financial position
- liaising between the board and homeowners and the professionals they engage (CPA, Attorney, etc.)

- Documenting the receipt and use of all association funds
- Assisting in the preparation and implementation of the operating budget
- Creating reports for the board of directors
- Provide information for preparing a reserve study and reserve funding plan summary.

The community manager may also perform non-financial duties for the association, such as

- A walk-through of the community to investigate the work of vendors and any violations committed by owners and tenants and to check the overall condition of the community and any issues that may need to be brought to the board's attention
- Conducting monthly or quarterly meetings
- Taking minutes of the meeting
- Initiating warnings, pre-liens, liens, and coordinating collections of delinquent owners
- Taking calls from owners for any issues that may unexpectedly occur between meetings of the board
- Coordinating vendors hired to work at the community
- Conducting the annual election of the board

SECTION 7

---◆---

MANAGERS OF ASSOCIATIONS

"Management is efficiency in climbing the ladder of success; leadership determines whether the ladder is leaning against the right wall."

STEPHEN COVEY

❖ The ABCs of Association Management

Compared to residential property management, where it is estimated that 70 percent of investment property owners self-manage their rental, in Utah it is estimated that 50% of the Associations self-manage. This statement generally has two exceptions: extensive associations and tiny ones. Extensive associations with one thousand or more owners hire their staff to keep the costs down. Only some associations with fewer than ten owners find adhering to all the laws cumbersome and prefer to stay below the radar and save the cost of management. But for everyone else, which comprises over 95 percent of all associations, it makes no sense to self-manage. Since board members cannot be compensated, or because they risk losing their insurance protection, and because the laws and statutes are so complex and time-consuming, associations find the best management company for their community. Residential property management and association management, although related in some respects, differ in Utah in three parts:

→ **No license required:** Anybody can manage your association. Someone just released from prison for grand theft can write checks from your operating account if allowed by the board. You do not even need a driver's license. In residential management, a property manager must have a valid real estate license and report any law violations to the Division of Real Estate (DRE). Anyone handling money for a property owner must also hold a valid real estate license. A person over 18 must complete 120 hours of pre-licensing coursework to obtain the license and then score 70 percent or more on the real estate license test. The real estate license test is complex, and 50 percent of those who take the exam fail it the first time. It is common for people to take it two or three times until they pass it. The DRE requires ongoing training, and the licensee must complete 18 hours of continuing education every two years. Not only must the property manager be licensed, but they must metaphorically hang their license with a real estate broker, who is liable for the conduct of that agent.

→ **No regulatory body:** No government agency oversees association management. For residential management, anyone managing a property must be a licensed agent who works for a broker or a broker and must disclose to the DRE that they are in the property management business. They are then subject to a random audit by the DRE, which usually occurs every seven to ten years. The DRE checks the trust account to ensure the broker has not commingled their funds with the clients' funds or, worse, taken any funds for personal use.

They also check the contracts, lease agreements, and other paperwork to ensure the broker complies with state law. If the broker is not in compliance, or there is something amiss with the trust account, a broker may pay a fine and, in extreme cases, lose their license and the ability to remain in the management business. Owners and tenants can even report a management company, which will trigger an automatic audit by the DRE to investigate the claim. No such regulatory body exists for association management. If an owner is unhappy, they hire an attorney and sue the board or the management company. Since management companies are consistently named as additionally insured by the association, they are suing themselves when they litigate with the association.

→ **No certifications required:** Many association management companies belong to either the Community Associations Institute (CAI), which is national in scope and can earn the designation of Association Management Specialist (AMS) with two years' experience, or the Professional Community Association Manager (PCAM) with five years' experience, or join the National Association of Property Managers (NARPM) and earn the Master Property Manager, MPM®, with five years' experience and 500 unit years under management. These certifications are friendly and provide informative classes to the participants. The tests required to obtain these certifications are straightforward, and the answers are easy since the tests are "open book."

Having the credentials shows some seriousness about the industry, which means the person who received the certification is qualified to manage your community.

❖ Picking a Management Company

There are hundreds of residential property management companies and property managers. Some manage just a few properties, and other thousands, but all share one commonality: they do not manage associations. But that is not entirely true. Ten percent of all residential management companies also offer association management services. Here are a few reasons why they don't always provide both services – property management and community association management.

A different set of laws: Property managers follow the state statute about tenant laws for residential management. The tenant has certain rights, such as quiet enjoyment of the property, and is entitled to health and safety, and the owner can expect the tenant to abide by the terms of the lease agreement. The property manager enforces the contract and protects the tenant. Association management is much more complicated and subject to several different areas of the law - the Community Association Act, the Condominium Ownership Act, the lengthy Revised Non-Profit Corporation Act, Tow Truck Provisions, Flag Amendments, Service Contracts Act, and Nuisance Laws. (That's 285 pages of law as single-spaced in a readable font).

Require new staff and responsibilities: Property and community managers are similar but different. The property manager makes decisions on behalf of the owner, such as how much money should be deducted from the security deposit at move-out, which tenant to select if a tenant or owner should be billed for a repair, and if a tenant needs to be evicted. The community manager does the bidding of the board. The board makes the decisions, and the community manager carries out those decision. They are more of a communicator and implementer. They assist the board, ensure the work performed by vendors is satisfactory, and inform the board when they are not. Each job has its pros and cons, but they are fundamentally different.

Lower profit per door: This is the most challenging hurdle for residential management companies. For a well-run company, between the monthly management fee, leasing charges, owner and tenant programs, and owner and tenant fees, one property can generate $250 or more per month. The net profit can be $25 to $50 per month, depending on the company and how efficiently they are run. In association management, my company's average fee per owner is $10-25 per month, with a net profit of $3 to $9 per month per owner. Association management is the "penny" business, so you must manage several pennies to make a dollar. You can make a decent living working five hundred residential properties; simultaneously, you will be in poverty, driving just five hundred association owners.

Boards at war: Most residential property managers manage properties in associations. They have first-hand experience with dysfunctional boards, unhappy owners, and incompetent association management companies that respond slowly to issues. They assume all association management companies behave the same way and want to avoid entering a business where mediocrity is the norm. In residential management, in many cases, where you have an owner who treats their rental as a passive investment and lets the management company make all the decisions, we may speak to an owner once or twice during the year. Mostly, there is no personal relationship with the owner of a rental property. There is no personal relationship with the tenant, and in fact, that relationship is more adversarial. Managing an association well means having a close relationship with the board and, particularly the president of the board. It means managing strained relationships when a board is at odds with each other or its members.

Poop, parties, and parking: Residential management has to deal with three *t's*: toilets, tenants, and troubles. That refers to constant repairs (toilets), difficult tenants, and constant issues with owners, vendors, and tenants. Association management has to deal with three *p's*: poop, parties, and parking. There is not a week that goes by for our community managers where they do not hear a complaint from a board member or an owner that someone did not pick up their dog's poop, there was a loud party until late in the evening by an owner or an owner's tenant, and due to lack of available parking, a car had to be towed or ticketed, and the car owner is angry. You can manage a hundred properties and, in certain months, have very few calls from tenants or owners. Still, if you work with ten communities and one thousand owners, there will not be a day that goes by without an issue from someone somewhere in your associations. Some call that madness; I call it job security.

❖   **The Three Types of Association Management Companies**

You need to find an association management company and want to find the right "fit" for your community and board. What are your choices?

1. Mom and Pop
For many years, this was your only choice. Until the proliferation of homeowners' associations in the 1990s. Most associations either self-managed or hired local small management companies. Now, these more petite "mom-and-pop" management companies specialize in
- Actively managing five to twenty associations
- Targeting ten to hundred owner associations
- Usually offering a low price
- Provide limited service and are available during work hours
- Outsourcing many functions such as collections, escrow, and elections
- Proximity to the association.

2. Mid-sized or Regional Company
This can be a residential and association management company

or a stand-alone association management company. They have built a "brand" and have the resources to manage more significant associations. They have the resources and technology tools of a larger organization, and rather than the "mom and pop" company where one person might do everything, this company will have dedicated departments for the different tasks needed for the association. Their differentiating factor will be that they are small enough to know your community but big enough to provide the necessary resources to manage it properly. Here are their traits:

- Manage 20 to 150 associations
- Target twenty members to two hundred owners in associations
- Provide most, if not all, services in-house
- Have departments for accounts payables, receivables, escrow, and collections
- Look for a long-term relationship with the board
- May have a central location and manage associations in a wide area
- Try to keep the same community manager with the same community for the long term

3. The Big Boys

Over the past ten years, there has been a trend for large statewide or multi-state companies to absorb the regional companies to grow their business and eliminate the competition. They offer a process over a person. They want to avoid a community attached to the community manager but, instead, like the board to appreciate their efficiencies and expertise on staff.

- Manage more than two hundred associations in the state and thousands in the country
- Prefer communities with 100+ owners
- Prefer communities with ample reserves
- Completely departmental, with all services in-house
- **Community managers manage one thousand to two thousand owners**
- Suffer from "churn" of community managers. Novice community managers start with more minor associations and are awarded more prominent communities and higher pay as they advance.

How Does the Business Work?

The board needs to understand how association management companies earn their profit and how they make their money.

❖ **Base Management Fee**

This is the fee charged to the association for the base services, such as monthly financials, attending the meetings, and coordinating vendors. Usually, the community manager is paid 20 to 30 percent of this fee for mid-sized and large companies as part of their compensation. The company may make a slight 10 to 20 percent profit on this fee. Interestingly, in association management, how they determine this fee is considered "proprietary knowledge." Only some companies publish their fee schedule and use historical information to calculate it. They have managed a similar-sized association, about the same agent with comparable monthly dues, so they charge a fee that covers their cost to operate and factors in a small profit margin.

Commonly boards will shop a this is a per door fee of $7.50 to $30 per door or homeowner depending on the size of the HOA. Now imagine that you have 50 doors in your community and your monthly fee is $7.50 per door that would equate to $375 per month and about $93.75 is going to the community manager. I am not sure about you, but I can't even go out to dinner and a movie with my wife for that. How am I to expect prompt return calls and results from a community manager that is supposed to manage the HOA?

Don't let the attractive per-door fees deceive you into thinking it's a bargain. Believe me, the management company will compensate for this elsewhere, as they can't sustain their business and hire skilled staff without doing so.

Here is how they make up that difference.

❖ **Reimbursable Expenses**

Anything mailed, sent, or done on behalf of the association

not included in the base management fee is reimbursed to the management company at their cost. Their cost will consist of both the physical and labor costs. Thus, a mark-up on these costs can create a nice profit for the company. They may charge an association $500 to create and mail a newsletter to the company at the board's request, but it may only cost the company $250. I have seen some managers charge a flat $50-$150 per month and label it as "mailing services" but it's not tied to the number of actual letters or statements that are created. Perhaps it is the fee to have the Pitney Bowes mail machine ready to go in their office should the need arise.

❖ Escrows

This is a large profit center for the Big Boy HOA companies. When an owner sells, escrow will demand a payoff of the dues; they may request the governing documents because the owner has lost them, and the new owner must be onboarded and transferred to the management software. The fee to do all this can be from $250 to $1,000. If a company manages 10,000 owners, they can expect 3 percent to sell each year or 300 escrows and $300,000 in additional revenue (assuming $1,000 per escrow fee). While the Mom and Pops and Medium Size Companies do make money here, it's not the same as they are managing less and most the times these systems are not automated.

❖ Late Fees and Collections

Owners tend to be late more often on their dues than they are with their mortgage because the consequences are less severe. They can avoid collections and a potential foreclosure until they are a few months in arrears on their rights. But a management company will typically take or share in the late fees with the association, charge for the pre-lien letter ($100 to $200), the lien ($200 to $500), and remove a lien ($50 to $200). The owner in arrears pays for this and not the association, so boards do not question this fee, and there is extra work for the management company.

❖ Bank Credits

Banks love residential and association management companies. Residential management companies hold in "trust" tenants' security deposits and legally cannot earn interest on these funds in Utah. Association management companies have reserves and operating accounts with the bank of their choice. Since these funds must be liquid and readily available to spend, the bank pays very little interest on these funds. To attract the business of management companies, banks will offer a monthly "credit" for all funds they have on deposit. This credit is a percentage and varies depending on the interest rate environment, net of interest paid to the association, and how strong the relationship is with the management company. The credit will vary but will generally offset the bank charges for checks, ACH, scanners, statements, and other bank fees. There is no such thing as FREE Checking for businesses. Association manager can make .5 to 1% of the balances. The credit can be used to pay bills related to management functions (accounting and software costs) but cannot include leases or payroll.

❖ **Different Departments**

Unless you hire a small "mom and pop" management company, you will be working with your community manager and different departments at the company. It is essential to understand what they do for your association:

- **Accounts receivables**: All funds the association receives, typically monthly assessments, one person receives. They input the amount paid into the management software and carry that forward if there is still an outstanding balance.
- **Accounts payables**: All bills are paid by this person for the association.
- **Finances**: Monthly financials are prepared by the accounting department. They reconcile all the accounts and check account activity. It is critical that this person not be able to access the account and write checks; otherwise, they could siphon off funds and cover their tracks.
- **Escrow**: When an owner sells, this person provides the

requested documentation to the escrow company and transfers the new owner to the system.
- **Collections**: If an owner is in arrears, they send out the warning letter, prepare the pre-lien letter, and record a lien if authorized by the board.
- **Elections**: The election process has become quite complicated, and it now takes over ninety days to prepare for and then conduct an election.
- **Compliance**: The operations department ensures the company complies with all state laws and ensures the company is adequately insured.

What Should You Look For in an Association Management Company?

Choosing the right management company for your association can be the difference between an enjoyable time on the board and a miserable one.

❖ **Monthly Fee**

What they charge for their services matters to you. All things being equal, if you can pay less and receive the same or a higher level of service and professionalism, that is better for the members. But remember, the most expensive word in the dictionary is "cheap." How did they get to this fee? If you request a quote from three companies, and one is drastically lower than the other, that may be a red flag. Also, please pay attention to the other fees they will be charging. Do they charge for mileage or meetings? One business model is to offer a low management fee but charge additional fees for every little activity. The best advice is don't pick the cheapest.

❖ **Reputation**

How other companies feel about this company now is a good indicator of how you will feel in the future. You should be able to talk to current board members to see their experience.

❖ Size

Do you want a large management company that may assign different community managers to your association over the years or a smaller company that can provide more intimate customer service and one manager?

❖ Fit

You are looking for the right fit for your community. The company should be interviewing you as much as you conduct your due diligence to ensure the business relationship is equitable.

❖ Location

You should expect the company to be somewhere within a reasonable distance to where your community is, but if your community manager lives and works an hour away, that may be problematic. I have seen community managers live in Spanish Fork Utah and manage associations in St. George Utah or even parts of Salt Lake City. Remember I don't find out about these until an unhappy board looks for another manager. Wouldn't it be wise to find a company that has a main office centrally located and to ask before where your community lives?

❖ Certifications

It is nice to have your community manager, or the management company certified, but they may need to be qualified to manage your association. It is easy to pass the certification test but does not reflect their capabilities.

❖ Their Magic Pixie Dust

Every management company can promise excellent customer service and a better experience than your current company, but how will they accomplish this? What makes them different?

❖ Their Business Model

How do they make a profit? What makes their business model

different than the typical company?

❖ Questions to Ask

No matter how professional looking the marketing material of the company you are interested in or how compelling the messaging is, you need to interview the company to ensure that marketing matches the reality. Here are some questions to ask and reactions you may have to the expected answers:

• What is your business model?

This is a simple question, and you should expect a direct response. They may specialize in significant associations with complex financials and many community amenities or smaller ones with lower expectations but who desire to comply. You want to know how they attract and satisfy clients with their services.

• What makes you different from the competition?

Another easy question to answer. It could be years in the industry, knowledge of the laws, location of the office, or high customer ratings from Google or Yelp. Still, every company is different, and they should be able to communicate that differentiation to you.

• Does your company manage residential properties or sell real estate?

Some association management companies only offer community management services. Other companies also provide residential services and help owners buy or sell real estate at discounted rates that help members. That in itself is not a bad thing but there can be some conflict of interests and the manager should be extremely experienced. Also, does the association management side of the business provide the resources it needs to service your community properly?

• What is the average number of owners in the associations you manage?

If the company specializes in communities with ten to fifty owners, and your community is three hundred owners in size, they may need more resources to accommodate your association. If they manage two hundred associations, and most are more significant than two hundred owners, your community of fifty may need to be made aware of the situation. Most management companies manage a range of association sizes but prefer a particular-sized association.

- What type of management software do you use?

The actual management software is optional. There are five or six excellent association management software choices available. Still, if the company uses no management software and relies on QuickBooks or Excel, that is a red flag. Their software should allow owners to pay dues online, submit maintenance requests online, and download governing documents. It should also enable the board to review financial statements online and read operational reports.

- Roughly how many associations do you manage, and how many of our size do you work?

This goes to the size of the company. A company that manages five hundred associations or one with fifty is fine, but your experience and expectations may differ significantly. If you have hired large companies in the past and had poor experiences, it may be time to pick a smaller company. If the small company needs more resources to satisfy your association, it may be time to go with a larger one.

- Can we cancel the contract at any time?

Most management company contracts are one year and then renew or convert to a month-to-month contract. If you wish to cancel that contract, you must give thirty, sixty, or even ninety days' notice. That is fine. Some contracts are automatically renewed for another year, and if you wish to cancel your contract, you owe management fees for the balance of that year. Some contracts also give the management company a timeframe to remedy any issues the board has with them. This is too cumbersome and an unnecessary hurdle and should be removed from the contract. The contract should be "at will" or every month after the initial contract period.

- What are your accounting controls?

Ideally, even if the company manages just a few associations, there will be a separation of duties, and the person writing the checks needs to be reconciling the account. There should be segregation of duties and rock-solid internal controls. This is the money they are handling.

- Does your company have an in-house maintenance department or ownership interest in any of the vendors you recommend to your associations?

It is not uncommon for management companies to own a maintenance or landscaping company. This ownership is neither good nor bad per se, but it could be a conflict of interest for them to use these companies unless they provide a competitive price with the same level of, or higher, customer service. It is also important the management company disclose this information up front to the Board of Directors. Telling the HOA that they will get a "discount" for services on landscaping if they use "ACME Landscaping" may be true but often, it's not a real discount as the company is owned or there is a revenue share agreement between the management company and the contractor.

- How many owners, on average, do your community managers handle?

This is a critical question for the company and the community manager assigned to your account. The company may say "no more than 1,000 owners." Still, since your community manager is so adept at their job, or another community manager left the company recently, they may be managing fifteen hundred to two thousand owners. Suppose a person is working in 25 associations with 1,500 owners. In that case, they must report to up to 125 board members and attend up to 50 community meetings per month with 25 hours of monthly walk-throughs, leaving no time to respond to owners and board members.

- What is the chain of command at your company?

If the board is not happy with the assigned community manager or the quality of work of the back office, to whom can they speak? Do you talk directly to the community manager or their assistant? Can you speak to the owner if you are entirely dissatisfied? The greater your access to the decision-makers at the company, the better it is for you.

- What are the transfer fees when selling?

Although the owners bear this fee and not a price paid by the association, it should be reasonable. Some management companies reduce their base management fees to secure the account and charge numerous or inflated ones. In Utah, the total escrow fees (transfer, demand, documents, etc.) should run from $200 to $400 per sale, however there are a few that charge up to $1000.

- How are collections handled?

It would help if you treated every delinquent homeowner equally, and ideally, the management company has an accounting department big enough for a dedicated collections person.

- How does an owner get a question answered?

What is the communication path if an owner has an issue and needs to get it addressed? Do they speak directly with the community manager, or is there a call routed to the correct department? What if there is an emergency on the weekend? How is that handled? The biggest frustration for many associations is the feeling that the level of communication dissipates once the contract is signed.

- Do your community managers have certifications or designations?

This is a "nice to have" requirement. Community managers do not legally need to be certified or have obtained industry designations to manage your association. Still, it shows a higher level of commitment to their profession and perhaps a higher level of professionalism.

- Can you tell us about the communication channel between the board and the community manager?

Can the board call the community manager directly? Can they speak to them evenings or weekends? How long a response time should they expect?

- What would you like to ask us or tell us about your company, and why should we select you?

Interviewing a management company is like going on a first date. Whether it is the owner of the company, or their higher level designate, you should be impressed with both their business and them. If you are impressed with them, it usually only improves when meeting the rest of the organization. The representative should be able to make a clear and compelling case for why you should hire them. Sometimes, it is not a good fit, and they will tell you so.

It is also just as important that you have the actual manager that will be assigned to your community. Too many times BDM's (Busines Development Managers or Sales people) will be the sales side but not the service side. The Association should get to know who they will be working with.

SECTION 8

MAXFIELD COMMUNITY MANAGEMENT

"There is no power for change greater than a community discovering what it cares about."

MARGARET J. WHEATLEY

❖ The Maxfield Community Management Difference

I write this book as the owner of Maxfield Community Management. I have written it better to educate potential buyers of properties in homeowners' associations, for current owners to better understand their role as a member, for board members to increase their knowledge of their critical job as a community leader, and to promote my company. I would be remiss if I did not spend some time explaining my company and our unique differences in the industry. I have never entered an enterprise, whether real estate sales, residential property management, or association management, to make a buck but rather to make a difference. We offer the highest level of service for the correct association at the fairest cost than any other association management company. This is how.

❖ Our Business Model

We hire licensed real estate agents or residential property managers who manage residential properties and associations for us. Each manager is limited to several association doors to ensure they can quickly respond to requests from homeowners and provide the very best customer service.

We are centrally located in Lehi, Utah, and have local "boots on the ground" where we manage associations. At the same time, the central office handles financials, accounting, operations, compliance, and back-office duties.

At Maxfield Community Management, we believe that exceptional community management isn't just about overseeing properties; it's about fostering strong, connected communities. Our commitment is to make HOA management seamless and efficient, allowing board members to focus on making impactful decisions while we handle the complexities. We strive to be the trusted partner that enhances the living experience for every resident.

Our pricing is not a mystery; it is even published on our website. We charge a flat fee per month per owner.

❖ Our Propitious Niche

We are a fit for communities with between ten and two hundred owners. Some of these communities are considered too small for the vast association management companies, who prefer associations with large reserves and match their economies of scale. Still, they are too big for the small "mom and pops" who do not have the resources or skills to service an association of this size adequately. We can manage associations from Ogden to St George because branch managers are already working "virtually" for us in residential property management.

❖ Our Community Managers

Our community managers are also our branch managers who manage up to a hundred residential properties for us through Maxfield Property Management, Inc. They are licensed by the Department of Real Estate and are considered independent contractors, which means they are not W-2 employees but receive a 1099 for income earned through their activities. They can only work for us but do not sit in a cubicle or clock in daily; their home office is their work office. We expect any branch manager who manages associations to earn their Certified Community Association Manager credential. We pay them 50 percent of the base management fee, which, on average, is double what the typical community manager earns. The other part of the fee is for the back-office support – our accountant and software costs. They manage up to five communities or five hundred owners, whichever comes first, so we expect higher customer service. This threshold is lower because they do have other obligations. There is no opportunity to be promoted to senior community manager, so if a fit exists, they may be with your community for many years.

❖ Our "Inside" Community Managers

If your community has fewer than fifty owners and

meets less than 4x per year and has no need for regular enforcement such as driving the community weekly, biweekly, or monthly, you will be assigned to one of our "inside" managers who is an employee of the management company. There sole work role is community management. This person has at least three years' experience in real estate or managing communities but, like our branch manager, is paid 50 percent of the base management fee and can manage no more than 900 owners or thirty associations. This is much less than the industry standard of 2000-3000 owners and 50-75 associations. Because we pay our members more, they provide a better experience.

❖ Four Performance Guarantees

We do not just promise to perform; we back it up with guarantees in your management agreement. If we do not perform as promised, we pay an accurate financial price:

- Response: If an owner or board member calls, emails, or texts, we will respond within forty-eight business hours, or we will waive $100 from that month's management fee.
- Vendor: If the board is not satisfied with the vendor's work we recommend and does not agree to complete the task to your standard, we will deduct $100 from that month's management fee.
- Service: For associations with more than fifty owners, your community manager will work with no more than 8 associations or five hundred owners. For associations with fewer than fifty owners, our inside manager will work with no more than thirty associations or nine hundred owners.
- Satisfaction: If you are unsatisfied with our service, you may cancel our management contract with a simple sixty-day notice.

❖ Transparent Pricing

Any association can easily calculate our pricing, and it is provided here on our website.

We have three service levels:

Level 1 - Accounting Only Plan

Level 2 - Core Advantage Full Service Plan

Level 3 - Club Max Plan

Each plan includes the basics:

- Prepare Operating Budgets
- Account Payables
- Account Receivables
- Monthly Board Accounting Reports
- Prepare and Distribute Notices
- Custodian of Records
- ARC Requests
- Home Owner Monthly E-Statements or Paper
- Member App and Portal
- Emergency Maintenance

The **Core Advantage Plan** is different than the **Accounting Only Plan** as it includes:

- Rule Enforcement
- Violation Tracking
- Recurring Maintenance Management

There are a few add ons such as Rental Tracking, Parking Enforcement and Club House and Ameity Management if your association has those.

Our full featured plan **Club Max** includes evertying above and includes the Clubhouse and Amenity Reservation System, Parking Enforcement, Rental Tracking and Non-Recurring Maintenance Management and Pool Management.

Here is s chart that gives a better picture of some of the service offereings:

Service	Essentials Plan	Core Plan	Club Plan
Online Voting	$150 Per Ballot	$100 Per Ballot	Included
Rule Enforcement	Hourly	Included	Included
Violation Tracking	Hourly	Included	Included
Clubhouse/Amenity Management	Not available	$90 per month Min or _____%	Included
Amenity Reservations	Not available	Included	Included
Parking Enforcement	Not available	Hourly	Included
Pool and Spa Management	Not available	Included	$90 per month Min or _____%
Rental Tracking	Not available	$90 per month Min or _____%	Included
Pet and Animal Registration	Not available	Not Included	$90 per month Min or _____%

Current pricing and offerings can be found on our website but our plans start at:

> Our **Accounting Essentials Only Plan** start from
> 3% of the Assesments - Minimum $250 per month
>
> Our **Core Advantage Full Service Plan** start from
> 4% of the Assesments - Minimum $350 per month
>
> Our **Club Max Plan** starts from
> 5% of the Assesments - Minimum $500 per month.
>
> www.MaxfieldHOA.com/pricing-plans

All plans have a $45 technology fee per month except the Club Max Plan where this included.

If you want a free HOA proposal please email us at info@MaxfieldHOA.com or visit our website MaxfieldHOA.com

But Wait...What if our Association is paying less?

> ❖ **The Two-Year Tiered Pricing Plan**
>
> The price you pay for monthly management services is essential to the board and the association's owners. You may

be paying less right now but are not satisfied with the service you are receiving. That may be why you are looking for a new management company. We provide a higher level of service at a fair management fee, but if you are paying less, you may be hesitant to hire us, even though our business model appeals to you. Because we want to be your management company and accommodating, we now offer a two-year tiered pricing plan.

If we both agree we are a good fit for your community, and your current base management fee is lower than our proposed fee, we will match that fee for the first year. After twelve months, we will increase our price to 90 percent of our quoted monthly fee, and after another twelve months, we will charge 100 percent of our quoted management fee.* If you are not satisfied with the service, we provide for the price you pay, give us a sixty-day notice, and you can cancel our management agreement at no cost.

Maxfield Community Management cares about the communities we manage and any increase in the management fee you may have to pay. With this tiered program, you may pay more over time, but your owners will appreciate the superior service they are receiving.

*For example, if you have fifty owners in your association paying $350 per month in assessments, according to our "Transparency Pricing" table, our fee would be $600 (50 owners × $12 per owner) and $350 (2 percent of $17,500) for a total base management fee of $950. If your current management fee is $800, you would continue to pay $800 for twelve months. In the thirteenth month, your management fee would increase to $855 per month (90 percent of $950), and in the twenty-fifth month, your fee would increase to $950.

CONCLUSION, ACRONYMS, & CONTRACT

In Conclusion

This book has helped you as a potential association property owner, current owner, or board member. State laws are constantly changing, and I suggest the board invest in a free book from a few law firms that will provide the current rules and regulations. I have presented the basic structure of HOA and how to have an enjoyable experience on the board if you are a director. At Maxfield Community Management, we strive to provide better association management services to boards looking for superior customer service at a fair monthly fee.

Feel free to visit our website for more information, www.MaxfieldHOA.com or www.HOAAccountants.com or reach out to me personally for more details at Derek@MaxfieldHOA.com.

Acronyms

ADR	-	Alternate Dispute Resolution
BOD	-	Board of Directors
CAI	-	Community Associations Institute
CAM	-	Community Association Manager
CC&R	-	Covenants, Conditions & Restrictions
COA	-	Condominium Owners Association
COI	-	Certificate of Insurance
DRE	-	Department of Real Estate
HOA	-	Homeowners' Association
IDR	-	Internal Dispute Resolution
POA	-	Property Owners Association
R&R	-	Rules and Regulations

Made in the USA
Columbia, SC
30 June 2024

37831086R00076